James I
Flo

James Phillips
Flood

Part I: From The Sea

Part II: Abundance

Part III: To The Sea

Part IV: New World

Bloomsbury Methuen Drama
An imprint of Bloomsbury Publishing Plc

B L O O M S B U R Y
LONDON · OXFORD · NEW YORK · NEW DELHI · SYDNEY

Bloomsbury Methuen Drama

An imprint of Bloomsbury Publishing Plc

Imprint previously known as Methuen Drama

50 Bedford Square	1385 Broadway
London	New York
WC1B 3DP	NY 10018
UK	USA

www.bloomsbury.com

**BLOOMSBURY, METHUEN DRAMA and the Diana logo
are trademarks of Bloomsbury Publishing Plc**

First published 2017

© James Phillips, 2017

British Library Cataloguing-in-Publication Data
A catalogue record for this book is available from the British Library.

ISBN: PB: 978-1-3500-6012-8
ePDF: 978-1-3500-6056-2
ePub: 978-1-3500-6055-5

Library of Congress Cataloging-in-Publication Data
A catalog record for this book is available from the Library of Congress.

Series: Modern Plays

Cover image © Sodium

Typeset by Mark Heslington Ltd, Scarborough, North Yorkshire
Printed and bound in Great Britain

To find out more about our authors and books visit *www.bloomsbury.com*.
Here you will find extracts, author interviews, details of forthcoming
events and the option to sign up for our *newsletters*.

Introduction

July 2016, Calais

'There's a girl, pulled up in a fishing net from the North Sea, naked. In the net a hundred migrants' life jackets. Her hands are bandaged. She's tattooed, a letter on each finger. The net's come from seventy metres down. She lives.'

I say this confidently. This much I know. And right now I've got nothing else.

I'm sitting in the front of a van with Alan Lane, driving towards the refugee camp at Calais: the famous camp that people call the Jungle. A few months from now the camp will be torn down, again. Half of it has already been demolished.

We're here to cook food for volunteers serving the camp, deliver supplies, and for me to research a project that at this stage I'm barely tracing the edges of.

In the van, Alan nods. At this point there's not much else he can do.

What do we know?

I've agreed a title: 'Flood'.

It's going to be one huge story in four parts: two full-length live plays, a short film and another thirty-minute play broadcast live on BBC 2. A big beast. It's not clear anyone has ever done anything like this. Probably for good reasons.

It's always like this, making stuff. Sky diving: but you invent the parachute after you've jumped out of the door, the ground getting big fast.

We spend a couple of days in Calais. Visit the volunteer base, go to the Jungle.

The Jungle is the wrong name for the place. Really it's the Front Line Club: West meeting East, Global North meeting Global South; us and them. I suspect our global problems can be found distilled into a precise liquid in each of the world's refugee camps. Everything you thought would be there is there: militarised French Police, day trip photographers looking for a buzz, naïve but magnificent volunteers. The camp split, voluntarily, into nationalities.

It's summer when we're there, so it's dry. When the rains come it'll turn Passchendaele pretty fast.

There's a makeshift church, where someone has painted a beautiful mural on some plywood. I photograph it. There's a white man in his sixties outside the church when I come out, chatting to Alan. He looks patient: I decide he must be a priest.

A few weeks back Britain has followed Farage and voted to leave the EU. I ask the perhaps priest why people want to come to a Britain that seems to detest them.

'They want to come to England because they have an idea of the place.'

February, 2017, on board 'The Chieftain'

I'm on a fishing trawler in the North Sea and apart from me pretty much everyone is vomiting. It's hard not to feel responsible.

We're shooting Part One.

Part One is pretty much precisely what I'd told Alan when we were driving to Calais: we're on the North Sea to drag a girl out of the sea.

It's been so rough that we've been shooting what we can in harbour.

But an hour ago the Captain of our rented trawler, frustrated at the impossible manoeuvring in port, snaps.

Alan approaches me, 'Fuck it, we're going out.'

So out we go, into the North Sea. And out we stay: because of tides and weather once we're out it'll be six hours before we can get back in again.

There's a brief moment of excitement. And then the first wave hits, and the casualties start. We learn fast that there are two types of sea-sickness sufferer: the cyclical vomiteers (one vomit and back in the game for ten minutes) and the long-term debilitated. The second category are lost for the whole voyage. Our editor finds a remedy: staring at the horizon and staying stationary stops the sickness. But you can't move, can't step away. She's like this, spell-struck, looking at the place the land meets the sky, for six hours.

I've been working pretty hard on *Flood* since summer. Parts Two and Three are written.

Large sections of it are in verse. Before this I've always thought there are enough constraints without the metrical. But something in the form of my recent shows makes the step logical: full of direct address, questions thought out loud in a public space. So the step from prose soliloquy to iambic pentameter – with phrases deliberately repeating, consciously shared – as the saga goes on, isn't a huge one. And more than anything sometimes it's nice to find a way not to write like yourself, trick yourself into new patterns.

In my head I called it 'The Storm', all the time I was writing Parts Two and Three. And it felt like there was something wild in it, something free. Touching on the places many things join: the migration crisis, religion, senses of place, belonging. I suspect it will, like some of our other pieces, enrage certain people on both ends of our political spectrum. Anything you write comes together when things which seem not obviously linked reveal their connections: the good stuff is often in the joins. But when you're navigating border country there'll always be trouble.

'Have you got a lighter?' Nadia Emam has appeared from a cabin in the depths of the trawler, where the waves roll you worst. Nadia's playing the Girl from the Sea, who has a name now: Gloriana.

She lights her cigarette, 'How's it going?'

I look over Nadia's shoulder. There's eight people vomiting off the side of the boat. Fifty per cent casualty rate, height of the battle. Nadia's blissfully unaffected. At this moment I consider whether she may actually have been sent from God.

On the train home I think about migrant ships in the Mediterranean: people crammed in, seas getting heavy.

April 2017, Hull

'The fucking thing has sunk.'

Alan Lane stands in front of me, dripping canal. He's wearing a dry suit and diving goggles. He's soaked. We're on site for Part Two.

'Thought it was meant to sink?' I offer.

'It's also meant to come back up again,' he says.

Our designer David Farley and Alan have built me what I wanted: a floating, see-through city on the huge canal basin where we are doing our live shows. There's a detention centre, a port and the House on the Hill. It's huge. The House sinks at the end of the show. Now we're testing our life-size toy. And sink the House does: but it goes down at an angle, fast, like it's been torpedoed. And once it's down, it stays down. Mired.

I should probably try to explain what I'm up to, beyond the adventuring of it all. From *The White Whale, Camelot: The Shining City* (two huge shows produced by Slung Low and directed by Alan) and onto *Flood*, I've been writing a new type of epic theatre. All three shows set in a similar world: a sort of future present. All shows deeply political but offering no easy answers. All shows high tech: we hear them through headphones as audience members, which allows both intimacy and distance all at once, long shot and close up in a single beat. All shows exploring big ideas but full of moments of spectacular: in *The White Whale* I asked for a boat that appeared from under water during the show and which then blew up like an oil rig at the end. In *Camelot* we started on the Crucible Main Stage and ended with a pitched battle between a cast of a hundred and fifty on the streets of central Sheffield.

Back on the canal, 36 hours pass during which the fucking thing remains sunk. It's snared on something on the bottom of the canal basin. We pump it full of air, to lift it. Alan, in his dry suit, makes repeated and ferociously heroic attempts to free it from the water. Nothing works. I can scuba dive and we're getting to the point where we're going to hire air tanks and approach the problem like a wreck dive.

Finally, deep into the second day, a new combination of rope positions, extra muscle and more air work, and the House rises. It sits there, on the surface, looking entirely cheerful about the havoc it's been wreaking.

A week later we try again.

I'm coming out of the office after working soliloquys with the cast. Alan's getting into his dry suit.

'What's happened?'

He puts on his goggles. 'Fucking thing's sunk again.'

It's clear we might need to think again about how we are going to achieve the end of Part Two.

June 2017, Hull

'So I'd like three camera boats to get in close and circle the caravan,' was what he'd said.

We'd been sitting in a Hull Gelato shop with Ross MacGibbon, the TV director for Part Three. We're about to shoot for the BBC. It's largely set on a sinking caravan, in driving rain, at the height of the flood. The English have become refugees. In virtually every way it's a technical nightmare.

Now we're back in our flat, late at night, discussing.

Thing is, we only have two free boats. And the water is full of ropes on which we pull platforms, a fishing trawler, ropes which snare around boat propellers.

We decide we can offer Ross one boat, but put two cameras on it. It's going to need some balletic skill manoeuvring that boat, and luck. If you hit a rope and snare, then the show stops. And of course there are actors in the water for large sections of the show. We've all trained and we've all got powerboat licences, but this is a big ask.

All eyes slowly settle on David Farley.

Farley's our best boat driver. And he knows best where the underwater ropes are.

'It's me, is it?' he says.

'It's you, Farley.'

One of the unique things about the conception of *Flood* has been the variety of different forms I'm incorporating. Part One is a short film and conceived like film: sparse dialogue, visuals written in as primary narrative motor. Parts Two and Four are plays for live performance and consciously theatrical: full of direct address, written partly in verse. Part Three is deliberately a hybrid: a 'stage' play written purely to be filmed; to be performed in 'one take' as a continuous show, containing verse soliloquy but also elements which will only work fully when finally seen on screen.

Two days pass. We're shooting.

David is manoeuvring a boat in a tiny space, trying to avoid sections of his own set as they pass through, whilst being pelted by his own rain machine. Adding to the picture is the fact that during the long months of *Flood* Farley has grown an enormous beard. Bearded, soaked to the skin, beset by his own creations: David Farley has become the King Lear of theatre designers.

I'm not laughing, though. Eventually we decided that we do need a second boat. And at that point the eyes settled on me. So I'm watching David from my own boat stage right, bobbing gently near the tempest.

During the pre-show reset I'd got caught on a line that had been accidentally raised to the surface. I'm told somewhere there's footage of me fighting to free the rope, my little boat rising forty-five degrees out of the water, a miniature *Titanic*. I don't think this happens to David Hare. Eventually we do some battlefield surgery, cut and retie the rope, the clock ticking. It's one of those nights.

But we get it done, cast and crew pushing themselves far beyond even the boundaries usually set for these huge shows. It's after midnight by the time we're off the water. Everyone's shattered, giddy, slightly shocked: the aftermath somewhere between that of a Press Night and a fist fight.

And Part Four is written too. I'm going into a reading of it now.

I find a deeply touching sense of emotion in the room: so many people have worked for so many months on a story without knowing the end. And now they will. I hope, silently to myself, that I haven't let them down. Good things only happen through the repeated work of a large group of people, each offering that extra unacknowledged hour day after day, week after week.

I'm often asked how you make things, where it all comes from. This year has been a fair reflection. One image – the girl in the fishing net – has finally, grudgingly, yielded a whole world, and I feel it could be taken further, in multiple directions. For the first time the scale of Four Parts feels like a restriction. I can see off shoots, can see Part Five, Six, Seven.

Which means, of course, it's time to stop.

James Phillips, July 2017

slung low

Founded in 2000, Slung Low is an award-winning theatre company specialising in making unlikely, ambitious and original adventures for audiences in unusual places such as on trains, in castles and shopping centres, with speed boats and on milk floats, in canal basins, through multi-storey car parks and across cities.

Recent work – on an epic scale using cityscapes as backdrops – includes *Mapping The City* (with iMove Yorkshire Cultural Olympiad in Hull), *Blood and Chocolate* (York Theatre Royal & Pilot Theatre), *The White Whale* (Leeds Inspired) and *Camelot: The Shining City* (Sheffield Theatres and Sheffield Peoples' Theatre). In 2016 Slung Low built a camp of artists who lived for a week in the grounds of the RSC, working with visiting public to create a ceremony that attempted to open the portal to the fairy world.

They have also produced two immersive adventures for children – *59 Minutes to Save Christmas* and (with Dep Arts Productions) *Emergency Story Penguin*.

Slung Low are supported by Leeds City Council and are part of Arts Council England's National Portfolio Organisations.

The company are based at The Holbeck Underground Ballroom (HUB) in Leeds – an open development space for artists and a place where Slung Low invite other companies to present their work that otherwise might not get to be seen in Leeds. All work presented at The HUB is Pay What You Decide. There is a dormitory for artists visiting the region and the equipment and vehicles of the company are lent to those who have need. It is a useful place that shares its resources with those artists who need them.

Artistic Director: Alan Lane
Producer: Joanna Resnick
Executive Producer: Laura Clark
Associate Director: Sally Proctor
HUB Programmer: Porl Cooper

www.slunglow.org

HULL 2017 UK City of Culture

Hull UK City of Culture 2017

Hull 2017 is 365 days of great art and cultural events inspired by the city and told to the world. The ambition is to create a nationally significant event that celebrates the unique character of Hull, its people and heritage. It offers a programme that takes in every art form, from theatre and performance, to visual arts and literature, to music and film, which goes into every corner of the city, whilst showcasing it nationally.

Working with local as well as national and international artists and cultural institutions, Hull 2017 draws on the distinctive spirit of the city and the artists, writers, directors, musicians, revolutionaries and thinkers that have made such a significant contribution to the development of art and ideas.

Renowned for presenting work outside conventional theatre spaces, each with a powerful, moving story at its heart, Hull 2017 commissioned Leeds-based Slung Low to develop their most ambitious and ground-breaking project to date. *Flood* – a four-part epic, told online, live in Hull and on BBC TV – was developed. A truly unique, multi-platform, theatrical event, *Flood* is the story of what happens when the world is destroyed, and how those who survive try to make it new again.

'A feat of logistics, Flood is likely to stand as one of the highlights of the year.'
The Guardian

Flood's epic adventures come to audiences in Hull and beyond with support from The Space, Arts Council England, BBC Arts and Spirit of 2012.

www.hull2017.co.uk

Hull 2017 Project Team
CEO & Director   Martin Green
Producer   Lindsey Alvis
Head of Production   Gareth Hughes
Head of Digital   David Watson
Assistant Producer   Martin Atkinson

Assistant Producer	Siana-Mae Heppell-Secker
Director of Communications, Stakeholder & Government Relations	Ben McKnight
Senior Publicist	Hannah Clapham for The Cornershop
Marketing Coordinator	Rachel Crow
Box Office & Visitor Experience Coordinators	Jessica Firbank & Jack Dunkerley
Audience Engagement Manager	James McGuire
Volunteer Programme Manager	Harriet Johnson

Flood

Flood

Flood, Part I: From The Sea

A Short Film

Cast

In order of appearance

The Captain	**Oliver Senton**
Sam	**Marc Graham**
Gloriana	**Nadia Emam**

Creative Team

Director	Alan Lane
Designer	David Farley
Composer	Heather Fenoughty
Sound Designer	Matt Angove
Producer	Joanna Resnick
Executive Producer	Laura Clark
Film Production Company	Sodium

For Sodium	
Director for Screen	Rob Booker
Producer for Screen	Phil Barber
Cinematographer	Matt Gentleman
Script Supervisor	Lia Hayes
1ˢᵗ AC	Andrew Barr
BTS Photography	Sam Conner
Storyboard Artist	Andrew Lamb
Editor & Colourist	Lia Hayes
Visual Effects	Peter Gee
Sound Mix & Design	Ray Hill

The Space

Commissioning Executive	Helen Spencer
Head of Audience Development and Distribution	Owen Hopkin

Flood, Part One: From The Sea was commissioned by Hull UK City of Culture 2017 & The Space.

The short film was released online on 27 February 2017 and toured to supermarket car parks across Hull for a week in an Airstream caravan.

Filmed on the North Sea and in Holbeck, south Leeds.

1. EXT. DAWN. NORTH SEA

The dark, empty sea, sun rising.

In the distance a storm, lightning coming down: a patch of darkness in an untroubled sky.

2. INT. DAWN. FISHING TRAWLER BASTION

*The cluttered cabin of a North Sea Trawler. The **Captain** sits at the table, oblivious to the motion of the sea. He is surrounded by papers.*

He is in his late 40s, tanned, dressed practically for the rigours of the cold sea. He is writing by hand, pen and ink.

*POV **Captain**: the page in front of him, a letter barely begun, written in his precise handwriting. 'Natasha –' and then a blank page.*

*The **Captain** hears a noise at the door to the cabin, looks up.*

*POV **Captain**: **Sam**, the First Mate, stands at the door.*

*The **Captain** conceals his letter under pages of hand-scrawled figures and business calculations.*

Sam   It's time.

3. EXT. DAWN. DECK OF FISHING TRAWLER BASTION

Wide: The fishing trawler alone and isolated in the North Sea.

*Now the **Captain** and **Sam** on the deck, surrounded by the machinery of the trawler. The **Captain** looks out to sea, sees the distant storm.*

Captain   Coming for us?

Sam   Leaving.

*A scarce shrug from the **Captain**.*

He leans over the side, looks down into the dark, shrouded waters.

Captain   Let's get on with it.

Now we see the machinery moving, hauling in huge nets from the deep. Mechanical sounds.

The first nets arriving.

Gannets and gulls circling, landing on the water: a dark swarm, looking for fish.

4. EXT. DAWN. DECK OF FISHING TRAWLER BASTION

The net rising from the sea. Empty.

The **Captain** *and* **Sam** *watching, on deck, unimpressed.*

Captain   No harvest.

Sam   What do we do?

Captain   Try again.

Captain *turns away.*

Sam   Lower the nets!

5. EXT. DAWN. FISHING TRAWLER BASTION

Close Up: The trawler winch heaving and spluttering heavily as it tries to pull up the next net.

Sam   Jammed!

The **Captain** *approaching the mechanism, a tool in his hand.*

Suddenly the winch starts to move quickly, pulling up the net with speed. The **Captain** *steps back, surprised.*

Sam   Net coming! –

And the net comes fast out of the water.

The net is empty of fish. Instead a hundred migrants' orange life jackets fill it. The **Captain** *moves towards it, shocked. He pulls at the net to release the bottom. The life jackets tumble out. Arranged within them, nestled in perfect symmetry, lies a naked girl, covered in tattoos. Her hands covered in dirty bandages. Dead but curled perfect like a statue. The* **Captain** *moves towards the heaped life jackets.*

Captain   Find something to cover her.

He reaches down to the dead girl. The cold skin at her throat. **Sam** *approaching behind him with a blanket, respectful, eyes turned away.*

And the girl sits up, blind eyes, vomiting out water, reaching for the **Captain**. *A howl coming out of her. Alive.*

6. INT. DAWN. FISHING TRAWLER BASTION

The girl sits wrapped in a blanket in the cabin. Unresponsive. Eyes unfocused. Across the cabin the **Captain** *and* **Sam** *watch her.*

Close Up: the tattoos on her legs, where they escape the blanket. Scales tattooed like a fish.

The **Captain** *moves towards her. She hears him, twists in her chair.*

Captain   She's blind.

Can hear us, can't see us.

(to the girl, in English) Where are you from?

Nothing from the girl.

Captain *(in Arabic)*   Where are you from?

Nothing. He takes her hands, makes soothing noises. With great delicacy he starts to unwind the bandages around her hands.

Captain *(to the girl)*   Let me change these dressings.

He unpeels the bandages. POV The **Captain**: *A letter fresh tattooed and still bleeding is visible on each revealed finger. No seeming pattern to the arrangement of the letters from his viewpoint.*

Captain (*to* **Sam**)   They're fresh, these ones.

Frightened, the girl pulls her hands away from him, raises them to her face, covers her eyes. Now this new placement of her hands allow the letters to be read correctly.

Close Up: Her hands over her face: 'G.L.O.R.I.A.N.A.'

Captain   Gloriana.

And now **Gloriana** *moves her hands left and right, exposing her previously covered eyes. Her eyes that have suddenly found perfect focus, found sight, now finding his eyes.*

He draws back, shocked. Standoff. And then **Gloriana** *reaches for him, afraid, grasping for warmth like a child.*

7. INT. DAWN. FISHING TRAWLER BASTION/ GLORIANA'S DREAM

Gloriana *lies huddled in the corner of the cabin. The Captain sits apart from her. He has been doodling on his pad. Next to the word 'Natasha –' now we see a childlike drawing of a mermaid.*

Sam *enters the cabin. They both watch her.*

Sam   The net was 70 metres down.

Captain   Tell no one.

Sam   She's sleeping.

We see **Gloriana**, *huddled under blankets, eyes closed.*

Now we slip into her dreams –

– **Gloriana** *floating in the deep sea, light distant, from above. Her eyes closed, like a baby before it is born, sound of distant noise distorted by water –*

– Now we return to the cabin. **Sam** *and* **Captain** *still watching her.*

Sam   What do we do with her?

Captain   Hand her in.

Sam   Where do we say she came from?

Captain   The sea.

– Now we return to **Gloriana***'s dream space, seventy metres down in the dark.*

And her eyes open, panic, swimming desperately, a net closing in –

Flood, Part II: Abundance

A Play

Cast

In order of appearance

Gloriana	**Nadia Emam**
The Captain	**Oliver Senton**
Sam	**Marc Graham**
Jack	**Naveed Khan**
Johanna	**Rani Moorthy**
Kathryn	**Sarah Louise Davies**
Natasha	**Lisa Howard**
Man A	**Dave Pattison**
Woman A	**Louise Brown**
Woman B	**Polly Pattison**
Peter Levy	**As himself**
Voice of RAF Pilot	**James Phillips**
Voices of the City	**The People of Hull**
Captain of the Jessica	**David Farley**

Chorus

Jane Aldridge	Les Curnow
Sean Alton	Gareth Davies
Janet Anderson	Sarah Firth
Nicky Austin	Nina Hanney
Ruth Austin	Barrie Jackson
Leanne Ayre	Sue Jarrel
Carol Baldry	Derek Kirk
David Beel	Sheila Leathley
David Bell	Shirl Lenton
Paul Benson	Chris Li
Grace Burnett	Steven Little
Louise Burnett	Katie McCreaddie
Sharon Burton	Stella McKendry
Tony Chappell	Debbie Mowforth
Linda Clark	Angela Needham
Sue Clark	Elly Pattison
Gary Crossman	Adam Peckitt
Clare Crowther	Pauline Phillips

Mhairi Rees
Tony Robinson
Sue Robson
Steve Roper
Jonathan Seymour
Ian Sykes

Mick Tite
Zoe Walker
Peter Whiteley
Louise Wildman
Alison Williams

Creative Team

Director	Alan Lane
Designer	David Farley
Composer	Heather Fenoughty
Sound Designer	Matt Angove
Movement Director	Lucy Hind
Associate Directors	Ingrid Adler
	Peter Bradley
	Sally Proctor
Design Assistant	Heledd Rees
Chief LX	Alex Johnston
Stage Managers	Calum Clark
	Olivia Dudley
Boat Crew	Hamish Ellis
Sound Deputy	Andy Sulley
Pyrotechnics	Doug Nicholson of External
	Combustion
Set Construction	SetFree Projects
Helicopter Pilot	Wayne Hedges
Chef	George Allison
Project Dramaturg	Kara McKechnie
Video Content	Sodium
Digital Producer	Brett Chapman
Producer	Joanna Resnick
Executive Producers	Laura Clark
	Jim Munro

Sheffield Chamber Choir

Directed by Robert Webb

Andrew Bailey	Louise Shield
Rita Belli	Robert Spooner
Michelle Doran	Cat Taylor
Matt Doubleday	Peter Taylor
Alan Heath	Kate Thompson
David Milsom	Peter Thompson
Ruth Milsom	Charlotte Winstanley

Flood, Part Two: Abundance was commissioned by Hull UK City of Culture 2017.

The play was first performed on 11 April 2017 in Victoria Dock, Hull.

Characters

Natasha, *the former Minister for Overseas and honorary Lady Mayor of the City by the Sea.*
Kathryn, *her daughter.*
Gloriana, *a girl found in the deeps of the sea.*
Johanna, *an Iraqi Christian.*
The Captain, *a fisherman.*
Sam, *his son.*
Jack, *an officer of the migrant processing system.*

Location: A City by the Sea.

'Flood'

Oxford Dictionary:

(Noun)

'**1.3** *literary: A river, stream, or sea*

2 *An outpouring of tears*

2.1 *An overwhelming quantity of things or people happening or appearing at the same time*

(Verb)

3. *Arrive in overwhelming amounts or quantities*
3.1 *Overwhelm with large amounts or quantities'*

At clearance –

Projected huge, on water.

Members of the community of the City by the Sea interviewed.

Black backdrop, single camera, no interviewer visible or heard.

Woman A   – What was it like? The City by the Sea? It was my home.

Wasn't rich. Not like it used to be, not Great like a hundred years ago.

It was its own place. It was proud. We were proud of it.

It was the end of the line, where the land stopped and the sea started –

Man A   – I lived on the edge of the dock and the wilderness. Where my father lived and his father. My father was on the ships and so was I, until the money ran out. Some of the lads went back when the whaling started again, for the oil you remember? The sea, that was always where the money had come from –

Woman B   – We knew it wasn't the greatest city in the world. It wasn't. But it was a city of the great world. Safe world. The logical world. Like Europe was, back then. The bit of the world where there were no more monsters under the bed –

Prologue

Gloriana *(V/O)*   Close your eyes.

Listen.

Voices of the City by the Sea, rising. Cell phone calls, radio shows, casual conversations, whisperings, shouting matches: the unacknowledged soul of the city melding together. A refrain we'll hear again and again and which can be fused with a musical refrain as we go on.

Gloriana (*V/O*)   Does he hear the world like this? Does he find pattern?

Then one radio signal coming out of the great melee:

Radio   – This is the fishing trawler Bastion we have a casualty on-board request emergency services over ... Repeat this is the Fishing Trawler Bastion approaching harbour we have a casualty on-board request emergency services over –

– Out of the melee of sound we find a single clear voice –

Captain (*V/O*)   She came to us one dawn. The girl. Far out
  one dawn alone beneath the wine-dark sea.
  One dawn hauling in nets from deep water
  From seventy metres down in the dark
  We pull up one net empty of all fish.
  In it one hundred life jackets
  Orange like those migrants leave on beaches.
  One hundred life jackets and a girl.
  Curled pale naked just bandages on hands
  A drownded girl. Tattooed. Dead but
  All her limbs arranged like a sculpture.
  Like someone high above had demanded order.
  Dead, no breath. My son the mate respectful
  Reaches to cover her. And she sits up. Alive.
  Grasping for warmth like something new born.

i.i

The **Captain**, *outside the Detention Centre.*

Now **Sam**, *his son, approaches.*

Sam   They want you.

Captain   Ok.

Sam   What will you tell them?

Captain   Little as possible.

The **Captain** *moves away from his son.*

Captain (*Turning back.*)   Unload the boat –

– Within the Detention Centre: A teenage girl with a tattooed body in a holding cell, her hands over her ears, head back. We hear the sounds of the city again, as she hears them, louder and louder. The room filled with light, blazing light, then black out –

– Shock cut into another room in the Detention Centre.

The **Captain** *stands at a window looking out towards the sea.*

Jack, *an officer in the Detention Centre, stands across from him.*

Jack   – She was dead?

Captain   Drownded.

Jack   – And then she wasn't?

Captain   Wasn't? –

Jack   – Dead.

Captain   She started to breathe.

Jack   You gave her CPR?

Captain   No –

Jack   – But she started to breathe?

Captain   Yes.

Jack   So she hadn't been in the water long?

Captain (*to us*) He didn't seem a man likely to believe in much. So I lied.

(*to* **Jack**) Not long.

Jack   But she was naked.

Beat.

Captain   Yes.

The clothes, they can be washed away. By the water.

Jack   Can they?

Captain   I'm told. When their boats sink.

Jack   All the clothes?

Captain   Perhaps.

Jack   Apart from the jacket?

Captain   The life jacket, yes. The ones the migrants wear.

Jack   Just one jacket?

Captain   No, many.

Jack   Many jackets but just one girl?

Captain   Yes.

Jack   So the others drowned?

Captain   Perhaps.

Beat.

Jack   There've been no boats this far north.

Beat.

Jack   Where's she from?

Captain   The sea.

Jack   Which country?

Captain   Don't know.

Beat.

Captain   Where is she?

Jack   You want to see her?

Captain   It's not a prison?

Jack   No.

Captain   They can't leave?

Jack   No.

Captain   It's not a prison –

Jack   – It's not a prison.

Beat.

Jack   You want to see the girl?

Captain *nods*.

Jack (*examining him*)   Because you saved her?

Captain *shrugs*.

Jack (*considering him*)   There is a doctor, now. But another day, perhaps.

The **Captain** *stands, starts to leave.* **Jack** *watching him.*

Jack   There've been no boats this far north.

Captain (*turning back*)   Situations progress, don't they?

i.ii

Gloriana – *the girl with the tattoos – sits huddled in the corner of her room in the Immigrant Detention Centre.* **Johanna** *enters, an Iraqi woman in her 20s.*

Johanna   New?

Gloriana *nods*.

Johanna   We will share the room then.

Where are you from?

Gloriana (*shrugs*)   Don't know.

Johanna   Muslim?

Gloriana *shrugs, shakes head*.

Johanna   You want to stay here? This country?

Gloriana *shrugs, nods.*

Johanna   In the detention centre where you come from is the most important thing. Outside the walls, no. In here, where you come from: it is the whole story. It is you.

Gloriana   I have no story.

Johanna   Why?

Gloriana   I don't remember.

Johanna   Nothing?

Gloriana (*unsure, illustrative with words*)   The water. A fisherman. Lifted me.

Johanna   A fisherman?

Gloriana   Yes.

Johanna *unsure what to believe.*

i.iii

– Music –

Now the **Captain** *walks away from the Detention Centre. He talks to us.*

Captain   Do you know it, the city by the sea?

It's my home, always my home, even when I woke far out to sea on the rigs, even when I dreamed divers' dreams, narcotic nitrogen dreams below the waves.

You know the dying docks, where once the world was brought? You know the new shopping centres, promising always more than they deliver? You know the Victorian centre, built when the world was ours and before the world forgot us? You know the place where the grey sky meets the grey sea? Where day by day the sea is taking back the land. You know the wilderness out where things were once made which now lies empty and where only the mad ones walk?

During this the **Captain** *walks from the Detention Centre, through the city, to the highest point of the place: the house on the hill.*

But the city when it is your city, it's more than this. It is us. Who we are now formed from who we were every then. The past: it's present, a place where you live haunted, each street a separate room in a memory palace, each step a motion through space but through time too until suddenly someday you can find yourself back where you began.

Now the **Captain** *stands looking up at the House on the Hill. He has walked into the shadow of a group of Protestors who look up at the house, becoming concealed in a crowd.*

Captain   This week, *she* has come home.

Illuminated within the house we see **Natasha**.

i.iv

Now we see **Kathryn**, *22, who stands within the House on the Hill, apart from* **Natasha**.

She talks to us.

Kathryn   This week Natasha, my mother, has come home.
Our parents: they failed, this much you know.
The world given them, promised us, the world of
Each generation rising, richer, easier, safe
More perfect, teeth whiter; each generation more
Like people in an iPhone advert: all done.
The world is dark and descending and afraid.

Natasha *calls down to* **Kathryn**.

Natasha (*to her daughter*)   The Protestors are back.

Kathryn (*to us*)   Do you know her?
My mother was Minister for Abroad,
For intervention, for democracy
Deposited down from twenty thousand feet,
For foreign wars, violence done to force good.

And then all that fell apart cause foreign wars
Caused torture in foreign prison cells and babies
got burnt by phosphorous, choked by dust.
And blood spilt abroad splashed up into eyes
At home and we could not see right or wrong.
And she – my mother – she was disgraced. So:
our parents failed. What price should they pay?

Now **Kathryn** *approaches* **Natasha**.

Kathryn   Mother –

Come away from the window. They'll see you.

Natasha   That's what they want isn't it, that frisson?

Kathryn   What they want is to take you to the Hague. Or
perhaps burn you. If they find a convenient stake along
the way.

Natasha   Is that what you want too?

Kathryn *silent*.

Natasha (*her little smile*)   Strange, to have found my
way home.

i.v

The **Captain**, *sitting near the House by the Hill. His eyes shut. The*
Captain *starts to sing, for himself, as he remembers –*

Captain   Look across the ocean of our love
   What do you see
   A new world one where we will be free
   We'll sail across that ocean, oh my love
   Just you and me, just you and me

   Look up at the darkling sky above
   What can you see
   The stars they'll speak to you in beauty
   There's a smiling face looking down my love
   On you and me, on you and me

Take my hand and dive beneath the waves
What will we see
Deep inside the heart of our mystery
And you know together we'll be saved
O you and me, O you and me

– Now lights up on a room in the Detention Centre. **Gloriana**
stands, shrugs off her blanket, head to one side, listening. She smiles.

Johanna, *across the room from her.*

Johanna   What is it?

Gloriana   Can you hear?

Johanna (*not understanding*)   No.

Gloriana   It is beautiful.

And **Gloriana** *sings, soft, in perfect unison with the* **Captain**.

Gloriana   And if we're ever forced oceans apart
    Where might you be
    I'll skim a stone across the wild sea
    And you'll know that you still hold my heart

As **Gloriana** *moves to complete the verse the* **Captain** *stops singing,*
lost in his reverie.

She smiles. She loves the song and the singing.

Gloriana   Cause I am you, and you are me
    you are me

Lights now on **Natasha**, *still in the House on the Hill far right*
across the City. And she can hear **Gloriana**. *And as* **Gloriana**
sings, soft smiling her first pleasure, **Natasha** *starts to sing softly*
to herself.

Gloriana/Natasha   And if we're ever forced oceans apart
    Where might you be
    I'll skim a stone across the wild sea
    And you'll know that you still hold my heart
    Cause I am you, and you are me
    you are me

i.vi

Gloriana (*sings*)   We'll sail across that ocean, oh my love
  Just you and me, just you and me –

Next day.

Gloriana *in a room in the Detention Centre. Head to one side. Hands bandaged still. She is calm. She is singing, in unison as we crossfade, the same song as the* **Captain**.

Now **Jack** *at the door, watching her sing. She is not embarrassed, has not learnt to be. Her singing fades.*

Jack   Don't know that song. What is it? It's in English.

Gloriana *half a nod.*

Jack   Yes?

Gloriana *half a nod.*

Jack   And you speak English?

Gloriana *silent.*

Jack   But you understood what I said?

Gloriana *raises her hand, half pointing at the air, like a tentative schoolgirl.*

Gloriana (*whispers*)   Learning.

Jack   Tell me about the Captain.

Gloriana   Captain?

Jack   Who brought you here.

Gloriana   The Fisherman?

Jack   Yes.

Gloriana   He took me up to the light.

Jack   – We know that people are being brought into the country, here, illegally. The further North the weaker our defences. Sealed into shipping containers, often. But there

are other routes. Trawlers meeting traffickers out to sea: we
have suspected this. If the Captain was involved in bringing
you from another country it is a crime, his crime: it is a profit
on misery. Which country are you from?

Gloriana (*wants to be helpful*)   I don't know what a country is.

Jack *turns to us.*

Jack (*to us*)   And so it began. Many days trying to solve a
puzzle whose pieces were scattered, rules of the game
ignored. Most of them, the migrants that come in boats,
hidden in lorries, concealed in containers: they know the
rules. They read them posted in Facebook groups: we
change a policy it's across a continent in a click –

Jack (*to her*)   Are you from Syria?

Iran?

Egypt?

(*In Arabic then English*)   How did you enter Europe?

Gloriana   I do not remember before.

Jack (*to her*)   Amnesia – forgetting – is no defence. If you
are fleeing war, perhaps. If you are fleeing persecution,
perhaps. But pretending to forget does not mean you
receive asylum –

Gloriana   – I am telling you what I know.

She turns away from him, silent.

Jack *talks to us.*

Jack   You think I'm callous doing this job? You know
there must be order. Half of you, your hearts bleed.
The other half, they harden. Half of you, you see
The poor, the fleeing masses as your children
You say 'suffer all the little ones come to us'.
The other half see their own sons and daughters
dispossessed, English futures wrapped

up and gifted away into foreign hands.
And is there real natural justice in that?
So, say I'm callous. But if there's no order
One day you'll look down from your high windows
Find the riot come tooth and claw to your street.

i.vii

Gloriana *sits with* **Johanna**.

Johanna *talks to us*.

Johanna (*to us*)   At first they ignored her, all these others detained. Left her sitting in the corner of the room, looking out towards the sea. But in the first days there was a little girl joy in her, before her dreams began. Her smile it spelled the word delight. The light, it glistened where she sat. I had been here many months, waiting for my yes or no. I wanted to teach her. She was thirsty for knowledge, like a soldier stumbled out of the desert –

Gloriana   – You came here why?

Johanna   I was not safe.

Gloriana   Why?

Johanna   Because of what I believed.

Gloriana   Why this place?

Johanna   Place?

Gloriana   Country.

Johanna   I had an idea of it.

Gloriana   What?

Johanna   That it was good. That it was fair. That it was safe.

Gloriana   What is it like? Outside the walls.

Johanna (*moved*) It is very cold.
   It is . . . there is so much. They have so much.
   It is the best place in the world.

The people, I do not know what they are thinking. Their
faces are written in a different language. They have lost faith
in themselves. They do not remember what they are. But I
believe in them even if they don't believe in themselves. I
believe one day they will protect us –

Gloriana   Us?

Johanna   – the ones who should be protected.

Gloriana   You lived outside the walls?

Johanna   A year. I am illegal. I was caught.

Gloriana   You want to stay?

Johanna   Yes. I pray for this. Will you pray with me?

Gloriana   I don't know. What is pray?

Johanna   You have a religion? Yes? Everyone does.

Gloriana *shrugs.*

Johanna   Don't remember?

Gloriana *shakes head.*

Johanna   It is what preserves people. Faith.

Johanna *stands, checks the room.*

Gloriana   What?

Johanna   Want to see no one is watching. It is dangerous.
To pray.

Gloriana   Why?

Johanna   Because it is powerful.

Johanna *reaches beneath her clothes and brings out a small silver
crucifix. Cradles it in her hands.*

Johanna   I will show you.

She shows her. **Johanna** *and* **Gloriana** *kneel. Lights changing.*

Johanna (*to us*)   Her smile it spelled the world delight. And so the residents begin to approach her. Eritreans, Syrians, Egyptians, Afghanis. This place in England, this centre: holds the whole world. They give her little gifts: these ones who had nothing but who had more than her, because they knew who they were.

i.viii

– The next day –

Detention centre. The interview room. **Jack** *across from* **Gloriana**.

Jack   The Captain. We believe he is involved in the trade in people. You first met him where?

Gloriana   The boat, I said –

Jack   – But this wasn't chance, was it, it was a rendezvous, it was arranged, he was expecting you?

Gloriana (*considers*)   Deep inside I think he was.

Jack   I don't know what that means.

And the girl leans forward and holds her bandaged hands over his heart.

Gloriana   In here.

Jack   No Jedi nonsense.

Gloriana   What is Jedi?

Jack   *Star Wars*. You know *Star Wars*? It's . . . excellent. (*laughs*) Like . . . they can move stuff with their mind.

Gloriana (*smiles, wonderful thought*)   With their mind?

Jack   – Doesn't matter –

Gloriana (*conspiratorial*)   – I know a secret about the Captain.

Jack   Tell me.

Gloriana   There's one (*indicates a tiny thing*) part of him that is still pure.

Jack   Pure?

Gloriana (*sits back content*)   This I know.

Beat.

Jack   Listen to me. The weakest always suffer: it will be you that suffers. You want to stay here then you must tell the truth.

Gloriana   Everything I know I will tell you.

Jack   Then tell me where are you from?

Gloriana *silent.*

Jack (*to us*)   Her face implacable. (*To her.*) Ok. We need a break.

Jack *leaves.*

Now **Gloriana** *smiles to herself. And she looks up and out and straight at us. We hear the sounds of the city again. She stands. She moves the chair that he was sitting on to the centre of the room. She looks at it, then she looks at us, smiles. A magician with her audience. Her smile. She puts her hands on her temples. She concentrates on the chair. Sounds of the City increasing. Her effort, increasing. After a moment the chair does not move. She looks up to us, shrugs, impish: to say, 'what did you expect?'*

Gloriana   Fail.

Now **Johanna** *in a different part of the centre.*

Johanna   She learnt the world not with her head but with her whole being. She learnt things so that once I had taught them I had somehow learnt them all over again, new –

Now **Gloriana** *joining her. In media res –*

Gloriana   The cities without kindness were to be destroyed?

Johanna   Cities of the Plain.

Gloriana   And He says, He bargains with Abraham, He says find me fifty good men and I will save the city, yes?

Johanna   But he could not.

Gloriana   Not find fifty?

Johanna   And he bargains again. Forty-five. And he could not find forty-five. And it goes on, fewer and fewer until they agree on the littlest number.

Gloriana   What was the littlest number?

Johanna   Ten. He will not destroy it for ten.

Gloriana   He could not find ten?

Johanna   No.

Gloriana (*leans back*)   I do not believe it.

Beat.

Johanna   The day the black flags came to our town they painted a red letter on each Christian House. Like an N. 'Nazarene.' We were to pay a tax for our belief or we would be killed. But it was a lie. We knew it was a lie. I ran. My friend, my neighbour, he stayed. Would not change. Would not tread on the face of Christ. They nailed him to a door.

Gloriana   Where was this?

Johanna   My home. The plains of Nineveh.

Gloriana   We could still have found ten. The littlest number. We will still find them.

Johanna   Perhaps. (*Smiles.*) The cities with no kindness, it is the Old Testament. Before Christ. Before he came to save the world.

Gloriana   A good man to save the world.

What if God had been silent? Would he have known to be good? Would he have known himself? Would he have been brave enough?

– time passing –

Jack *outside now, talking to us as he is walking back into the room.*

Jack (*to us*)   There was something about her. I'd go home each night and of all the hundreds in that centre, all those waiting for a yes or a no, it was only her face that travelled back with me, only she that swam the river of my dreams. I was told she woke in the night, screaming. (*to* **Gloriana**) What is it you dream about?

Gloriana   The storm.

Jack   Because of the television? (*To us.*) The news was full of strange reports, unexplained storms in the east, a sudden relentless weather beating down on countries far away. (*To her.*) Because of that? Or because of something you remember –

Gloriana   It is coming, coming here –

Jack   What is?

Gloriana   The storm.

Jack (*smiles*)   These things are thousands of miles away.

Gloriana   No: they are in you.

Jack (*to us*)   We watched her, we who must decide, watched to see if she was actually part of a group. To catch the moment when she dropped the act. It never came.

And then one day: the fire.

Fire spreading through the detention centre.

In their room, **Gloriana** *and* **Johanna**.

Gloriana   Look. Smoke.

Smoke is rising. **Johanna** *moves to the door, looks.*

Johanna   The building is burning.

Music. Sound of the fire, of screams building.

Johanna (*crying out*)   Help! Help us! (*to us*) And the girl, she closes her eyes, as if she is making maps in her head, hearing out the space –

Gloriana   – No one is coming.

Johanna   Help us! Please!

Gloriana   Come with me.

Gloriana *takes* **Johanna**'*s hand, leads her out into centre.*

Now **Jack** *as the detention centre burns.*

Jack (*to us*)   Don't know who did it. Us or them? Masked men wanting to burn out foreigners? The foreigners themselves? Some days self-harm, it is their best protest. Don't know –

The fire huge now.

We see **Gloriana** *moving through flames,* **Johanna** *coughing, leaning on her.*

Johanna (*to us*)   And the dark is coming for me, I can't put one foot in front of the next, flames building and we come to a locked gate and we will die –

A locked metal gate.

Johanna (*to* **Gloriana**)   No no no.

Johanna *sinks to the ground, overcome with smoke.* **Gloriana** *walks up to the locked gate, kicks at it, pushes. It doesn't yield. Now she rages at it, shakes the metal, animal roar. She stands back. Looks across to the other woman.*

Gloriana   Johanna. Johanna.

Johanna *murmuring, broken.*

Gloriana *sinks back on her haunches. Then stands. Confronts the locked gate, ten feet back from it. Closes her eyes. Concentrates. The flames raging around her. An explosion. The gate opens.*

She drags the woman through to the other side, away from the fire. Kneels by her, sees that she is breathing, eyes open.

Gloriana   You're alive.

I must go now.

Gloriana *stands and disappears into the night.*

Now the next day, **Jack** *outside the gutted Detention Centre.*

Jack (*to us*)   We were lucky, not many died. But in the chaos many fled. After the fire engines and the news crews and the ambulances we found an absence among us, an empty chair by a window.

The girl from the sea was one of the disappeared.

ii.i

Natasha *at the window of the House on the Hill, looking out.*

Natasha (*to us*)   It becomes my evening hobby. Watching them. The ones come to register their protest. To see how deep into the dusk they remain. Those with the most endurance I admire. Although I don't yet know if their endurance is in proportion to their virtue.

They always stand – because of the law is it? – far enough away that their faces are like memories, smudged by distance. I cannot make out an individual face.

And then one night: the girl. The girl who stands apart, who stands still when all the others have left. Standing still when I go to bed. And the next night and the next. Each day no closer to joining the crowd, each day separate.

Tonight: there she is –

We see **Gloriana**, *alone outside the house.*

Alone, an urchin looking up at lights.

And now she holds out her hands, palms unobtrusively held upwards, her head leaning back and it starts. It starts, slowly O so slowly, to rain.

– Build in a moment across the city with other characters acknowledging the rain? Umbrellas, opening, hoods going up? A beginning –

She doesn't move away, doesn't try to cover herself. And she was just the littlest thing, not dressed for rain and I was up and walking and out the door. First moment in years I had no fear, although we were warned always of assassins, I knew I would be safe –

Natasha *leaves the house, picks up a blanket on the way, and now stands in front of* **Gloriana**.

Natasha (*to her*)   Are you cold? You must be.

The girl nods. Says nothing. Her face, it's like I know her, like I dreamed her once and then woke up forgetful but here she is, complete.

(*To her.*) 'Who are you?'

Gloriana *holds up her hands, slips out of the loose bandages, presents them.*

Natasha   On each finger of her hand was a letter fresh tattooed into her skin.

(*To her.*) I don't understand. Who did this?

And she then lifts her hands, places them over her eyes, their position reversed. And the letters spelled –

(*To her.*) Gloriana. Is that your name?

Gloriana *shrugs.*

Natasha   Why have you come? And serious face she started to sing, soft, simple, for herself –

Gloriana (*sings*)   And if we're ever forced oceans apart
Where might you be
I'll skim a stone across the wild sea
And you'll know that you still hold my heart –

Natasha   – the song that I had sung that night, that only he and I knew –

Gloriana*'s song fades away, gentle.*

Natasha   Do you have somewhere? To go?

Gloriana   No.

Natasha   Come inside.

ii.ii

Natasha *and* **Gloriana** *in the house.*

Natasha   She sat in the corner of the room, next to the window where you can see out to sea. And I knew who she was, my ghost –

Gloriana   Thirsty.

Natasha *hands her a bottle of water and the girl drinks it, greedily.*

Natasha   Where have you come from?

Gloriana   There was a fire. I left.

Natasha   The immigrant centre?

Gloriana   Yes.

Natasha   Why did you come here? To me I mean. You know who I am? –

Gloriana   He loves you.

Natasha   Who?

Gloriana   The Fisher Man.

Natasha *moves away from her.*

Natasha   How do you –

No one could know that.

I haven't seen him since I was . . . someone else.

Who do you work for? The newspapers?

(*softening, believing*) Does he?

Gloriana   I wanted to understand.

Natasha   What?

Gloriana   Love.

Natasha   Love?

Gloriana   I have been listening. It is what I liked to hear.

Natasha   What he did say?

Gloriana   He hasn't said it out loud, he –

Natasha   – Wait.

Natasha *sees* **Kathryn** *approaching.*

Natasha (*to* **Gloriana**)   My daughter is coming. Don't say any of this to her –

Now **Kathryn** *is at the door.*

Kathryn   Who's this?

Natasha   Her house burnt down.

Kathryn   Ok.

Natasha   She was outside. And it started to rain.

Kathryn   Ok.

Natasha   I asked her in.

Gloriana *draining the last part of the large water bottle, noisy.*
Holds the bottle up and smiles.

Kathryn   Ok.

Natasha (*to us*)   And in this way Gloriana entered my
household.

ii.iii

The Docks.

Sam *is moving boxes and equipment taken from the Trawler*
Bastion. The rain is still relatively light. **Jack** *approaches.*

Jack   Your father here?

Sam   No.

Jack *waits,* **Sam** *continues to move equipment.*

Jack   She's missing. The girl. (**Sam** *ignores him.*) The fire. At
the centre. You read about it? (**Sam** *still moving boxes.*) And
she disappeared. Your girl –

Sam   – Not my girl.

Jack   Migrant girl, I mean. The one you took on your boat.

Sam   Know who you mean.

Jack   Any idea where she's gone?

Sam   Why would I?

Jack   Your father brought her in.

Sam   – and then you took her.

Jack (*shrugs*)   Where's your father?

Sam   At sea.

Jack   Weather's not great.

Sam   Think we only make money when the sun's shining?

Jack   You look for other ways to make money?

Sam   Like what?

Jack   Bringing people into the country perhaps.

Sam (*stops*)   We done here?

Jack   Sure. (*Stands.*) Couldn't place her. The girl. She said she couldn't remember who she was.

Sam   Lot of them say that, don't they?

Jack   Lot of them?

Sam   Ones on the boats.

Jack   On the boats?

Beat.

Jack   No. They all got stories. All want to tell them. How they get what they want. Just her: she's the only one who's an absence. She say anything to you?

Beat.

Sam   Nothing.

Jack *moves to leave.*

Sam   Tattoos were pretty special. See 'em?

Jack (*shrugs*)   Sure.

Sam   Scales on her legs.

Jack   Scales?

Sam   Like fish skin.

Jack (*considers*)   Tell your father I'm looking for him.

Jack *leaves.*

Sam (*to us*)   You trust him? (*shouts*) Father! Father! (*to us*) He's hiding.
    I listened to the rain last night. Did you?

The beat of that wild rain on my bleak house.
My bleak house in my bleak street. Dying City.
How many lay last night and despaired
Solitary, listening to the rain?
I thought of my mother. Died. Tumor. Found
Too late for our too slow hospital. Fail.
He sat silent, corner of the room, no words
For her when she was going. Double Fail.
My father thinks he knows the world. He doesn't.
He doesn't even know this country, his home.
Drains are clogged with discontent. Dirty water
Rising ready to flow out into the street.
Since the Kingdom ceased to be united,
None able to go down into the shit
To root out the blockage with their own hands –

The **Captain**, *who has been concealed, enters.*

Sam He's gone. The girl. She's disappeared.

Captain Disappeared?

Sam Escaped.

Captain *nods, non-committal.*

Sam They burnt them out. The Detention Centre. She ran.

Captain You blame her?

Sam That net was seventy metres down. How can she have lived?

ii.iv

The House on the Hill.

Natasha *moving through the house.*

Natasha – First night she wakes screaming. I reach the door to the room: sudden silence. I lean in, hear a sound like choking, like an infant trying to form words. My hand on the door knob. Then nothing. Just her breathing. I'm in the corridor like when Kathryn was a baby and I was swaying praying 'sleep little one please sleep'.

I don't go in. Does she hear me, in her dream? Is she comforted?

Same pattern next night and the next. Caught on the threshold –

But the days were a delight. I found myself doing things I'd never done when my children were small. I cooked for her. Really. Opened a recipe book. Sat next to her on a sofa to see what she was reading. And she read *everything*.

My heart had been an empty space. But suddenly it was abundant. It was full again. A child: it teaches you to see the world again, fresh, does it not?

Natasha *now downstairs,* **Kathryn** *coming in, taking off her rain coat. TV on in the background.* **Gloriana** *asleep on the couch.*

Natasha   Ssssh –

Kathryn   – Not sleeping through the night, your waif and stray?

Natasha   You don't know what she's seen.

Kathryn   Do you?

Natasha   No.

Kathryn   Who is she?

Natasha   I don't know.

Kathryn   Trying to redeem yourself?

Natasha   What do you mean?

Kathryn   Taking her in. Orphan Annie. Will we be telling the press or a priest? Is it your soul that troubles you, or history books –

Natasha   – It's not that –

Kathryn   – you'll be a peace envoy next –

Natasha   Kathryn. (*Looking at the TV.*) What's that? Turn it up –

TV   '– Unprecedented scenes from Istanbul where last night a tsunami struck the ancient meeting place of east and west. At this moment we cannot confirm what remains of this great city once known as Byzantium' –

Sounds of the City.

Gloriana *is at the door.*

Gloriana   It's begun, hasn't it?

Natasha   What has?

TV (*V/O*)   '– we are also receiving reports of colossal storms moving west from Asia Minor towards Eastern Europe –'

– Sounds of the City –

iii.i

The City.

Music building through all this scene –

First the House on the Hill, **Natasha** *moving through the house –*

Natasha   One night the screaming did not stop. I followed my usual pattern. To the threshold and waiting. Hand on the door. But tonight it doesn't end, ancient sorrow like the song of whales. On and on. And I push through the door –

– **Natasha** *enters the room –*

– and see her squirming on the bed, a creature tortured on a table. I move to her, lie on the bed, curl myself around her, the smell of her hair, soothe 'little thing, little girl lost, baby child', words like swaddling clothes and the sadness it seems to quiet for a moment and I lie back and let the breath out. Relief. Silence. Close my eyes. Then drip drip drip, water strange persistent on my face. I look up and the room is crying, that's my first thought, the room is crying, and there is water flooding down from the ceiling –

– *water pouring down within the room??!* –

– not a pipe bursting, water somehow formed within the room, water weeping down on me from every surface and I think of a scripture lesson long ago when someone said 'is god silent cause he weeps for us and he has no words left only tears', O the water coming down and I knew it was somehow to do with her –

Gloriana *sits bolt upright.*

Gloriana   The sea. Something terrible is happening.

Snap LX – > Now across the city: The Docks.

Sam   This was the night of the shipwreck –

Snap LX – > Now the burnt-out Detention Centre.

Jack   – The weather it had been worsening through the week, vast winds blowing in from the east –

Snap LX – > Now the **Captain** *moving to stand near his son.*

Captain   – at first it was radio chatter –

The sounds of the city now, as **Gloriana** *moves down out of the House on the Hill and into the open and from the sounds of the city a radio signal becoming clear –*

Radio   – This is Coastguard Clipper Drake we have unidentified traffic unresponsive a mile out, over –

Gloriana *outside the house. Sounds of the city.*

Gloriana   – They're sinking. Can you hear them? The water's rising, at their ankles now –

Now **Kathryn** *at the window of the house –*

Kathryn   – She was tormented, the girl, an animal smelling danger on the wind –

Now **Natasha** *coming out of the house after* **Gloriana**.

Natasha – What is it? What have you seen –

Gloriana – You have to help them, you have to help them –

Natasha Help who?

Gloriana The boat.

The **Captain** *at the docks, binoculars, looking out to sea –*

Captain There!

Sam What?

Captain Heading towards the rocks. Can't avoid them now –

Visible now: out to sea there is a big fishing trawler, sinking, blown and battered by the wind and waves.

Gloriana (*to* **Natasha** *as she exits the house*) Fire.

Captain – O Jesus no, hold steady hold steady –

Sam – What is it?

Captain They're going to hit.

The trawler crashes into rocks out to sea.

Natasha A fire where?

An explosion on the floundering ship, seen across the city.

Gloriana *starts to run across the city, towards the docks and the sea.*

Natasha Where are you going?

Gloriana To them.

Natasha *follows her.*

Sam What can we do?

Captain We're the ones here. (*To* **Sam**.) We can try.

The **Captain** *and* **Sam** *move towards a little boat.*

Jack   It's been raining for a week now, without pause. Each day heavier. Tonight: hail hammering loud on houses, the people of the city turning up television sets to drown out the noise. So they did not hear when the drowning started. But we saw the sudden light out to sea, the first explosion from the boat and then –

Another explosion.

Music building.

The **Captain**'s *boat heading out towards the shipwreck, bouncing across the waves.*

Out to sea, the ship floundering on rocks.

Jack, **Natasha**, **Kathryn**, **Gloriana** *on the shore.* **Jack** *separate,* **Kathryn** *separate,* **Natasha** *closer to* **Gloriana**.

Jack   The people of the City becoming aware now, aware that something terrible was happening here –

Natasha   – People reaching for binoculars, for cameras with long lenses, trying to see out across the waters, seeing for the first time the desperation of those living other lives –

Kathryn   – how are people people when they know their end is here? Do they reach out for the arms of strangers? Do they cry?–

Jack   – and this place, this country, this city by the sea: it is somewhere you read about disasters not somewhere you can see them with your own eyes –

Captain   – felt my heart slowing like the moment you know a fight can't be avoided, battlefield feeling, and our boat bounces over waves towards fire –

Jack   – we watched as waves did what waves do, tore down what men had made, what men dreamed –

Natasha   – I looked across to *her,* the girl, the only one not looking out to sea, the only one who stood with her eyes closed –

Gloriana (*her tattooed hands over her eyes*) – I could see them could see them packed so close they could not move see them covered with piss with shit hollering out fear in the dark, alone, waiting for the long night and I thought no, not tonight –

Sam – Migrants, hundreds, packed like animals to the slaughter –

Natasha And the girl walked down to the sea shore, and she knelt. Waves vast in front of her, she knelt –

Gloriana *on her knees. Sounds of the city mingling with the swell of the music.*

Now the little boat reaching the rocks, light of a helicopter above, weave helicopter chatter into soundscape –

Sam And we are here now, trying to come alongside, rocks and a shattered ship wind and waves beating us away –

Captain – Trying to hold a small boat steady in a great tempest and my son moving to the prow of the boat, trying to reach out –

The boat making attempts to get close and to save them.

Sam – and they were so close, the doomed ones, dead already even when they're screaming out life, just an arms-length away, I could see their faces smell the stench of them, so close like we were the same but *no* that arms-length was a thousand miles, it was the distance between having a future and becoming the past –

Captain – And again and again the waves pushed us away –

Sam – And again and again we went back to be pushed away –

Captain – but it was too far. We could make no bridge. They could not be reached.

The little boat turns away.

Natasha   – And now she stood, the girl. Opened her eyes, stood and she ran at the water, at the waves, at the sea and it yielded. It yielded to her, it opened to her –

The sea parts.

Gloriana *running through the waves.*

Natasha   And she ran through waves held high above her. Ten feet, twenty feet forward was it? And then a wall of water in front, impassable.

Gloriana *still surrounded by the waters.*

Natasha   Ten feet into the tempest: is that how far faith can carry us?

And the waves came crashing down and swept her back to shore.

And I looked to my left, my right expecting to see crowds, people fish mouthed hooked by awe. But it had passed unremarked, the miracle.

Natasha *moves to the girl, now sodden at the sea shore.*

Natasha   Of all those there only I had seen it.

Kathryn *at the sea shore now, approaching.*

Natasha   Kathryn!

Kathryn   What happened?

Natasha   The waves.

Kathryn   What did she do?

Natasha   She wanted to save them. Take her. Take her back.

Kathryn *takes* **Gloriana**.

Natasha   Go!

Kathryn *and* **Gloriana** *moving back towards the house.*

Now **Sam** *and the* **Captain** *at the sea shore, soaked, free from their boat.*

Helicopter light passing overhead.

Sam (*to us*)   It was chaos on the shore, emergency services running for boats, bodies floating in now from the water, the people of the city out from houses sudden misery tourists in their own streets and then like a rope thrown perfect through the crowd I saw –

Captain   – (*to himself*) *her.*

At this moment father and son caught and held by the sight of two separate women, in separate directions.

Sam (*to the* **Captain**)   Dad, look, the girl –

Sam *has seen* **Gloriana** *leaving the scene on the shoulder of* **Kathryn**.

Captain   – (*to us*) there she was. Overcoat oversized drowning her, older so much older but still it was her –

The **Captain** *has seen* **Natasha**.

Sam (*to the* **Captain**)   Dad, the girl from the sea, I saw her. Dad!

Captain *doesn't take his eyes from* **Natasha**.

Sam (*to the* **Captain**)   You see the girl?

Captain   No. I –

Sam   Come on! Let's find her.

Captain   You go. I'll follow.

Sam (*considers his father*)   Alright.

Sam *leaves.*

Captain (*to us*)   I walk along the sea shore towards her. Her face lit by the fire from a sinking ship. Looking out to sea, lost. My hands are shaking, these hands, that have held the wheel steady in forty-foot seas. 10 feet now, five, and I remember her nineteen years old standing on this sea shore and the taste of her still in my mouth, five feet, I reach out touch her, casual ignoring all the decades past, reaching for her like she'd just turned away at a party and I was ushering her attention gentle back to me –

He touches her.

Captain   And it was now.

She turns. Looks at him for a long time. Smiles.

Natasha   Matthew.

Captain   Yes.

Time passing.

Dawn.

Now **Jack** *walking down a line of body bags.*

Jack (*to us*)   At dawn a surprise –

Sam *joining him.*

Sam   Look at them.

Jack   What?

Sam   The migrants. Can't you see what's wrong?

Jack (*to us*)   It took me a long time to see it, concealed in plain sight.

Oh.

They were white, every one. The drownded.

European, every one.

Born Christian too, I suspect, every one.

Sam   They weren't running from a war. They were running from the storm. It's come for us now.

Beat.

Sam   We should talk.

Jack   About what?

Sam   The girl.

iii. ii

The next day.

Gloriana *walking through the city, hoodie up, talks to us, the rain coming down –*

Gloriana   You want to know what I am? So do I.
  This much I know: I am a something
  Trying to become a someone. Like you are.
  Like you have been each every day of your life.

Wrapping the rain coat around her, looking up to the skies.

  Dark waters are rising in your souls.
  The ones from the sea: could not be saved.
  Is this to be allowed?
  The storm is coming, and it will find us,
  a plane through blue sky into a high tower.
  But there is love. I know, I have heard it.
  And if there is love there must be an answer.
  That's what you believe, in the West, is it?
  Right now you think the rain is done to you
  Right now you think the rain is separate
  But understand this: you too are liquid
  Which means you too may be implicated.
  Which means that you too may not be fixed;
  You too are liquid: which means you can change –

Kathryn *is running after her.*

Kathryn   Where are you going?

Gloriana *turning away.*

Gloriana   Want to find out.

Kathryn   What?

Gloriana   Who I am.

Kathryn (*to us*)   I had followed her through the city. She stops now, by the water, looking out towards the sea.

(*to the girl*)   How will you?

Gloriana *looks out to sea, silent.* **Gloriana** *turns back to* **Kathryn**.

Gloriana   How do you find out who you are?

Kathryn (*serious, honest*)   I don't know –
  I haven't learnt how to do that.
  Let's learn how.

Gloriana   You will help me?

Kathryn *holds out her hand.*

Kathryn (*to us*) And so we began. Our little quest. To make a lost one found.

iii.iii

Kathryn *and* **Gloriana**. *The House on the Hill.*

Kathryn *talks to us.*

Kathryn   First internet searches. Every country from which migrants were pouring. Pictures, phrases from foreign languages, paintings, pop songs – you ever heard middle Eastern pop music, woah, – or religious chants, anything that might spur a memory, anything that might tie her to a place?

Then libraries, largely because she loved the silence of our City's dwindling, empty library. Histories of amnesia, of the effects of trauma, of drowning: multiple possible plot lines for a mystery into which she could not place herself.

A long journey which revealed no holy land, no place of origin. Just the scale of a global crisis I had not grasped:

65 million people are displaced, 1 in every 113 people currently living on this little O, the earth.

And this before the storm.

And then one day –

Kathryn (*to* **Gloriana**, *across the room*)   No memory before the boat?

Gloriana   No.

Kathryn   What do you like?

Gloriana   Like?

Kathryn   To eat, to wear, to do?

Gloriana (*considers*)   I like your mother's food.

Kathryn (*unimpressed*)   Never cooked for me.

Gloriana   I like your clothes. This scarf. I like this.

Kathryn *is wearing an 'ethnic' scarf.*

Kathryn   My mother says I dress like a Palestinian. That I'm an ambulant political gesture.

Gloriana (*doesn't get the joke*)   Not at all. There was a Palestinian in the centre. He had no scarf.

Kathryn   Ok.

Gloriana (*shrugs*)   I like to listen.

Kathryn   Who told you your name?

Gloriana *holds up her hands, as before.*

Kathryn   That's how you know your name?

Gloriana *shrugs.*

Kathryn   You know who did this to you?

Gloriana   No.

Kathryn   We're going to buy you some gloves.

Gloriana   It is ugly?

Kathryn (*smiles*)   It's badass.

Gloriana   What is badass –

Kathryn   Tough.

Gloriana *stands, pull her t-shirt over her head, not self-conscious.*

Gloriana   I have these.

Tattoos down her back, intricate. **Kathryn** *looks, then turns her head away.*

Kathryn   You're beautiful.

The girl smiles, is struck by this. She moves and sits close to **Kathryn**.

Gloriana   Look. These are better.

Kathryn   Better?

Gloriana   Not tough.

She offers **Kathryn** *her back to examine.* **Kathryn**, *shyly turns back to her. Reaches out a hand, touches.*

Kathryn   These ones are faded, like they should be carved on a wall.

Gloriana   Yes.

Kathryn   What are these symbols, over and over –

Her fingers tracing the patterns on the girl's back.

Gloriana   – can't you see –

Kathryn   No.

Gloriana (*turning to her, and mimicking a fish mouth*)   Fish.

Kathryn   – fish! Like a child would draw.

Gloriana *kisses her, the fish mouth transforming.*

Kathryn *accepts the kiss for a second and then moves away.*

Kathryn   No.

Gloriana   No?

Kathryn   I'm too old for you.

Gloriana   How old are you?

Kathryn   22.

Gloriana   I am so old I have faded. (*Points to her back, smiles.*)

Kathryn   I'm too fortunate, I will not take advantage of you.

Gloriana   Too fortunate to kiss?

Kathryn   It's not like that.

Gloriana   Show me yours. Your marks. Lift up your sleeves.

Beat.

Gloriana   I know they're there.

*Now **Kathryn** lifts her sleeves. Welts from where she has cut herself visible.*

Gloriana   Did that to yourself? Cut yourself, hot knife? Yes.

Come back to me. I want to learn by tasting. Come back to me.

*And **Kathryn** crosses the room to her and **Kathryn** yields to her.*

Kathryn (*to us*)   Later I watched her sleep. She did not cry out from her dreams that night.

(*to the sleeping girl*) You're powerful and you don't know it. Because you're your own, completely. You're powerful because you're parentless: you can make yourself up.

In the morning she woke and said –

Gloriana   Is there a Church?

Kathryn   A church?

Gloriana   I want to go to a church. That's next.

iii.iv

The Detention Centre.

Jack *and* **Sam** *in a room.*

Sam   Why do you think it's happening?

Jack   What?

Sam   The storm.

Jack   I don't know. No one knows. It's weather.

Sam   Were you at my school?

Jack   Your school? No. Didn't grow up here.

Sam   Thought not.

Jack   You've come here to talk about the weather?

Sam   The net was seventy metres down.

Jack   The net?

Sam   We found her in. The girl.

Jack   Alright.

Sam   Seventy metres. Two hundred feet, more. Gets dark down there. Freezing –

Jack   – why are you telling me this?

Sam   She couldn't have lived. Couldn't have done it.

Jack   She did.

Sam   Yeah.

Jack   People dive deep.

Sam   With safety ropes, with safety divers, with fucking rebreathers. Not a girl in the North Sea, naked –

Jack   – I don't believe that she came out of the sea. I believe you were trafficking her. And something went wrong. Maybe she tried to run. Swim. You put hands on her?

Sam   You think that you're an idiot.

Beat.

Jack   So what do you want?

Sam (*leans forward*)   Something's wrong.

Jack   Ok.

Sam   And she's to blame.

Jack   The girl?

Sam   She's the why. She came here – next day, next fucking day, it all starts to fall apart. Next day the rain. There's something not right with the girl.

Jack   She's not here any more.

Sam   I know where she is.

Jack   Where?

Sam   Who she's with. The daughter of the politician. You know the one? Dresses like a refugee –

iii.v

The sea shore. The **Captain** *stands looking out to sea.*

Now **Natasha**, *approaching, talking to us.*

Natasha (*to us*)   I knew he would be waiting. And where.

Matthew!

He turns to her.

Natasha   Here.

Captain   Yes.

Natasha   You did not forget.

Captain   No.

Natasha   I tried to.

Captain   Forget me or –

Natasha   Both.

Failed.

Beat.

Captain   Your life. The things you did.

Natasha   Angry?

Captain   I don't mean the war. I mean –

You went away and the world it was yours. You meant something.

Natasha   Some days, perhaps.

Captain   I would sit here. Every year. Same day.

Natasha   I have never been back here. Or never left, one of the two.

Sit with me?

He nods. They sit on the sea shore.

Natasha   And how was it, your life? Heard you were a diver.

Captain   Yes, once. Rigs. Deep. Around the world.

Natasha   You found someone?

Captain   Yes. I did, yes. She died. It was bad.

But she was not you.

God, it is good to say that. No, not good but *good*.

Natasha   I'm not me anymore.

Captain   No?

Natasha   Perhaps now, with you.

Beat.

Captain   This rain.

You knew I would come for you?

Natasha   A girl told me.

Captain   Daughter?

Natasha   No. I have a daughter though –

Captain   – I read –

Natasha   – but not her. You read that?

Captain   In the newspaper. They blurred her face, like they do for famous people's children. Looks like you, does she?

Natasha   No. Well her face maybe, but she is . . . not like me. She *doesn't* like me.

Captain   Of course she does –

Natasha (*deep feeling*)   – once she hurt herself. Because of me.

Captain   Because of you, you can't know that –

Natasha   – Oh I do. Year to the day, after the first invasion in the desert. Year to the day, she did it. Nearly lost her. No one knows.

The **Captain** *reaches his hand the distance to her shoulder.*

Natasha   My whole life started here, this piece of ground. Wrong. I buried one life here.

(*Whisper.*) She's here. Under here. Like a miracle in reverse.

Captain   Yes.

Natasha   Our child. O, our child.

Natasha *lies down on the earth, coveting it.*

After a moment the **Captain***, Matthew, lies down next to her, embracing the woman and the earth.*

Natasha   Come to the house, will you?

Captain   Yes.

Natasha   Meet the girl.

Captain   The girl?

Natasha   She knew. She knew you had not forgotten. I think she is an angel, sent.

– They walk through the city –

iii.vi

They have reached the House on the Hill.

Captain   It's the oldest house in the city. Beautiful.

Natasha   You know I'm the Lady Mayor? Of the City?

Captain (*teasing*)   Lady Mayor?

Natasha   Former politicians, they give us ceremonial things: so the loss of actual power doesn't cut too deep.

Captain   Comes with a house does it, the ceremony?

Natasha   Yes.

Captain   Not bad.

Natasha   She's not here.

Captain   Your daughter?

Natasha   The girl. It's odd. Feel I can't breathe when she's not around –

Now **Kathryn** *coming in the front door, smack into the* **Captain**.

Kathryn   Who are you? (*to her mother*) Inviting more people to live with us?

Natasha   He is my friend. From before.

Kathryn   Before?

Natasha   When we were young.

Kathryn   There was such a time, was there? (*to the* **Captain**)
What was she like, 'before'?

Captain   Beautiful.

Kathryn   Ah, that sort of friend.

Natasha   – Kathryn –

Kathryn (*to the* **Captain**)   – don't worry, my father won't
walk in. He's been absent since the Inquiries started and
things all got a bit Richard Nixon –

Captain   – I'm not worried.

Natasha   Where is she?

Kathryn   She?

Natasha   You know.

Kathryn   My mother has located a new and improved
daughter.

Natasha   Was she with you?

Kathryn   Coming. She wanted to stay longer in the church.
She's very devout suddenly, particularly for someone with
such extensive body art.

(*to us*) – I had left her, my little one, hours before, in the
white church, where once the whalers prayed, where the
slavers sang. She was distant to me, suddenly, foreign and
far away, in that bright white stone room –

(*to* **Natasha** *and the* **Captain**) So were you school sweethearts?
Was there like a foreign interventionist society and your eyes
met over a volume of the collected catastrophes of Henry
Kissinger –

Gloriana   – They were in love. There was a child, born
dead, a lost one. Buried by the sea, yes?

Gloriana *is at the door, her approach unnoticed. Music soft,
building.*

Natasha   Yes.

Captain   This is the girl?

Natasha   Yes.

Captain   I know her.

Gloriana   He brought me up.

Kathryn   What do you mean?

Gloriana   He was the one. The fisherman. In the sea.

Kathryn   You? You found her?

Captain   Yes.

Kathryn   Was it you, carved into her hands?

Captain   No.

Kathryn   You know who she is though –

Captain   – No.

Gloriana   *I* know.

Kathryn   Who you are?

Gloriana   Why I'm here.

Natasha   Why?

Gloriana   To save the world. Look.

Gloriana *points out to sea.*

Kathryn   And we looked out, across the water. A thousand little boats on the sea, approaching. Tiny lights in the darkness, looking for answer. (*To* **Gloriana**.) What is this?

A thousand little boats on the sea, distant, light within them.

Gloriana   The storm. It has reached France, Holland, Denmark. They are looking for a place of greater safety.

Now a hammering on the door of the house.

Kathryn   Who is it?

Gloriana   The son. His (*the* **Captain**) –

Natasha   – Your son –

Captain   – I don't know.

Gloriana   Let him in.

Now **Sam** *entering the room.*

Sam (*to his father*)   You found her?

Captain   No. Just chance.

Sam *is holding his phone. He sends a text. Across the city,* **Jack's** *phone lights up. He starts moving.*

Captain   Why are you here?

Sam   Her.

Captain   What have you done?

Sam   What have I done? What have you done? You brought her here, to this country. You brought them all here –

Natasha   Brought who?

Sam   Do you know this man?

Natasha   Yes. I do.

Sam   We meet them offshore. Mile offshore, more, we meet them. Our boat meets a bigger boat. And they come alongside and we take 'em. Eighty, ninety, hundred a time. Don't know where from: their skin it says Africa, Middle East. Thousand pound, two thousand a soul. We trade in souls, don't we, father? We trade in souls. And then into port, before dawn, and two hundred grand's worth of souls disappearing into the city streets, unknown, unremarked.

We did this to England.

But one day, just fishing, proper day proper work, one day: there she is. Naked and inked and coming up in a net. Drownded but alive.

(*Indicating* **Gloriana**.) This one. This one brought the weather. This one brought the storm.

What have *I* done? What have we done?

Beat.

Natasha (*ice*)   Let me be the politician again. True, this?

Beat.

Captain   Yes. Forgive me.

Natasha (*to* **Sam**)   The storm. What does it have to do with her?

Gloriana *has moved to the window.*

Gloriana   The boats, they're getting closer.

Sam (*to* **Natasha**, *to the others*)   She is not like us. Is she? Don't lie. Is she? You know don't you, what have you seen –

Natasha   – Why not?

Sam   Seventy metres down we found her.

Captain   Doesn't mean anything –

Sam   – You joking?

Captain   It's cold down there. Can stop the heart. Body knows that, slows you like you're dead but you can live, cold lets you live, once I was working deep, diving, welding, there was an explosion the tube that kept warm water in my suit blew out, fifteen minutes till the rescue diver but I was so cold, so I lived –

Kathryn (*to the girl*)   Is that true? The cold? Is that how it was?

Another hammering on the door.

Gloriana   No.

Jack *enters with immigration officers in tow.*

Sam   I found her.

Natasha   Who are you?

Jack   I work for the city.

Natasha   Why are you in my house –

Jack   You know this girl?

Natasha   Yes.

Jack   So do I, to shelter her it is a crime –

Natasha   – do you know who you are talking to –

Gloriana   – Wait all of you.

And they freeze. Sounds of the city.

Kathryn   – Later I would think of that moment. It wasn't that I couldn't move. It was that someone had suggested it was wrong, that it was *inappropriate*. Not suggested to my brain, but to my nerves, to something animal inside. Like a sudden, brief, stilling poison. And we stood still, all of us, and she just walked out, free, my love, out into the night –

Gloriana   It is time for me to go.

The little ships are here now.

And **Gloriana** *walks out of the House on the Hill.*

Kathryn   A thousand tiny boats, a refugee's Dunkirk, approaching –

Far off, in a different light we now see **Johanna***, in the Wilderness.*

Johanna   And we were waiting for her, far out in the Wilderness, where they say the mad ones walk.

Gloriana *walking towards* **Johanna** *and the Wilderness.*

iv.i

Projected huge, on water.

Again members of the community interviewed. Black backdrop, single camera, no interviewer visible or heard.

Man A   We were overwhelmed. A thousand ships. And everything, it was happening at once, you won't understand this but when everything starts to happen at once, when everything starts to just *go* the things that might be possible . . . Can't be done.

Woman A   You think we didn't try at first? You think we didn't try?

Every one of those thousands, those tens of thousands, the European ones . . . We took them in. Filled the University gymnasium with them. The school halls. Shopping centre.

The theatre: that was the first mortuary I think –

Woman B   Wasn't enough.

They were desperate, can't blame them but can't let it go either. They were hungry, there wasn't enough, started stealing I heard.

French, Germans, Belgiums: in the end what did they have to do with us?

Man A   And then the first cataclysm. The rains, they had been getting worse, day by day. And one day the banks of the rivers burst. The waters spreading. Bridges swamped, roads impassable. And we were cut off. The city by the sea was an island. We led back to ourselves.

Woman B   We took them in. Before we sent them out. You should remember that. Write that down.

iv.ii

One week later.

Sounds of the city into sound of helicopters above.

Snap in media res, the House on the Hill. **Natasha** *and* **Jack** *in the room. A phone ringing incessantly.*

Natasha   – You will not do this.

Jack   I won't?

Natasha   You will not send these people out.

Jack   And what power do you think you possess to stop us?

Natasha   I have placed a call. To London.

Jack   This city will collapse if we do not do this.

Natasha   You send them out it's already all gone.

Jack   You people. Your phrases, your idea of yourself: do you understand we're not a country anymore, we're an archipelago, cut off?

Enter **Kathryn**, *holding the phone.*

Kathryn   It's London.

Natasha *takes the phone, moves away from them.*

Jack *looks out the window.*

Jack   The wall's going up.

Walls being built around the City by the Sea.

Kathryn   What will happen?

Jack   Food will come to us, inside the walls, from helicopters. We'll ration it. What we do not need we will send out to them in the wilderness.

Kathryn   There won't be enough.

Jack   For a while there will.

Kathryn   And then?

Jack   Either we starve or they do.

Kathryn   It's over, isn't it?

Jack   What?

Kathryn   England.

Natasha *re-joins them.*

Kathryn   What did they say?

Natasha   The barrier on the Thames. Gone. Water like a wall they say. We've lost control of the South Coast.

Kathryn   Who's in charge?

Natasha   Crisis management is devolved back to local authorities.

Kathryn   What does that mean?

Natasha (*simple*)   Government is collapsing.

(*holds out the phone to* **Jack**)   They want to talk to you.

Kathryn (*indicates* **Jack**)   He's in charge? The ones like him?

Natasha   Yes.

Kathryn   The barbarians are inside the gates then.

Mother, what will you do?

Natasha's *hand still held out, the phone in it.*

Kathryn   You'll stop him, won't you?

Natasha's *hand still extended. She lowers her head.*

Jack *steps forward, takes the phone from* **Natasha**'s *hands.*

He leaves the room.

Kathryn   You'll leave us to them? Leave her to them? That's your bravery, your tough choices?

Natasha   I don't know what I can do.

Kathryn   It was this part of you that started the wars, this part of you never blinked when they drowned people on the water-boards, this part of you gave away our goodness because you stood by –

Natasha   – Sometimes goodness exists because we will allow terrible things. We believed we could remake the world, make it free –

Kathryn   Was it your goodness that put the bombers out over the desert?

Natasha (*simple*)   Yes.

It is not easy.

You children do not get to judge. You don't get to judge hands made dirty keeping yours clean. You are weak, all of you children weak –

Kathryn   – You did not make that good world though, did you?

Kathryn *moves to the window.*

Kathryn   She's out there.

Natasha   Yes.

Kathryn *moves to the door.*

Natasha   Where are you going?

Kathryn   To find her.

Kathryn *leaves.*

Natasha   Kathryn! Kathryn!

Natasha *hesitates, then dials a number on the phone.*

Now a visual moment, the refugees being moved out of the central part of the City by the Sea, a great torrent of people on the march.

Hymn 'The Day Thou Gavest Lord Is Ended'. **Kathryn** *joining the throng.*

Hymn   The day thou gavest, Lord, is ended,
the darkness falls at thy behest;
to thee our morning hymns ascended,
thy praise shall sanctify our rest.

> As o'er each continent and island
> the dawn leads on another day,
> the voice of prayer is never silent,
> nor dies the strain of praise away.

The makeshift walls going up.

> The sun that bids us rest is waking
> our brethren 'neath the western sky,
> and hour by hour fresh lips are making
> thy wondrous doings heard on high.

> So be it, Lord; thy throne shall never,
> like earth's proud empires, pass away;
> thy kingdom stands, and grows for ever,
> till all thy creatures own thy sway.

And now the wilderness is walled off.

Now lights on the **Captain**.

He stands at the wall, looking out over the wilderness, the exodus.

Captain   What is the wilderness? Literally
it's the place we no longer make things,
The place of connection where factories
Once stood, through which the whole world once flooded,
Abundant. Now husked, hollowed out,
Shattered buildings open to the skies.
Decades now home only to the dispossessed.
But now it is full again, all the people
From a thousand little boats, all of Europe
Drenched huddled in a thousand little tents.
Abundance come sudden to a darkling plain.

iv.iii

The office of the burnt-out detention centre. **Jack** *on the phone.*

Jack   Yes. Yes. The supply drop will be secured. We have
weapons, yes –

Puts his hand over the phone and talks to us –

Jack   – There's a people's militia on the wall. If we hadn't allowed it, they'd have done it anyway. The people. The situation is developing hourly. There are days when order, when the world, needs men on the walls with guns. You know that. Know it deep down. You ready to serve?

Sam *is at the door.*

Jack   You want me?

Sam *nods.*

Jack   Where's your father?

Sam   Don't know. Really.

Jack   You should be in prison the both of you.

Sam   Got time for that?

Beat.

Jack   What do you want?

Sam   Men.

Jack   Why?

Sam   We need to get the girl.

Jack   Get her?

Sam   Kill her.

Beat.

Jack   Why?

Sam   You know why.

Jack   We kill her this ends?

Or you just want to do it?

Sam   You want me to go out there and say what I know –

Jack   – what you know? –

Sam   – what we saw, where she comes from, that she's the reason?

Want me to shout that in the street, think you'll hold the city once they know that?

Jack   – You don't know that's true –

Sam   – They'll be like wolves heading out of those gates with knives and bats –

Jack   – no one will believe you –

Sam   – here, now, today they'll believe anything. Anything gives them hope, anything gives them back control.

Jack   Hope's what you want is it?

Sam   Control's what you want.

You'll help me?

Jack (*defeated*)   How many men?

iv.iv

The Wall.

Night.

Sam *is leaving the City Walls. Enter the* **Captain***, who has been concealed by night.*

Captain   Wait! Wait!

Sam *pauses. The* **Captain** *approaches, passes out of the Gates.*

Captain   My son.

You're going out? Out there?

To find her.

You'll bring her back, will you?

Examines his son's face, close now. He puts his arms on his son's shoulders.

Captain   You must not hurt her, Sam.

Anger rising in **Sam***. He hits his father hard in the stomach, in the face. The* **Captain** *collapses.* **Sam** *kicks his father on the ground, repeatedly, spits on him.*

Sam   You don't understand, do you? I have seen them. You have shown me them. Packed into a ship so close in the dark they can't see their neighbour but can hear their screams their prayers, stand there swaying coated in someone else's vomit. They're in my dreams. If we don't do something about them, about this, then do you know what will happen? It will be us in their place. It will be us in the dark.

Sam *walks out into the wilderness.*

The **Captain** *struggles slowly to his knees.*

Captain (*to us*)   He doesn't see it. Chance of miracle from something new, something introduced. The grit that might yield a pearl from the oyster. He sees an entry wound, sees a splinter suppurating into a sore.

iv.v

The Docks.

The **Captain** *sitting by the sea.* **Natasha** *enters.*

Natasha   Your face.

Captain   Yes.

Natasha   Who did this?

Captain   Does it matter?

Beat.

Natasha   I need you.

Captain   For what?

Natasha   My daughter has gone out into the dark.

I have let her down. In my life. She thinks.

She might be right.

I don't want to fail. Fail her.

Captain   You'll go out?

Natasha   Yes.

Captain   You think things can be saved?

Natasha   Will you help me?

Captain   Why me?

Natasha   You cannot say 'no'. You are the last left who cannot say 'no'.

The **Captain** *considers. The* **Captain** *stands.*

Captain   Come on.

Natasha   How can we get past the wall?

Captain   We don't need to. The sea.

He moves towards the little boats in the harbour.

iv.vi

The wilderness.

Sounds of the city.

Johanna *talks to us. An encampment/shattered building in the Wilderness.*

Gloriana *approaching as if in flashback, then moving through time in the scene. People coming out of shells of buildings, to witness.*

Johanna   She came to us one night. The girl. Far out
    One darkling night onto the empty plain

She came to us. We who had been waiting,
Waiting for this. Did she know it? Did she
See the little fish tattooed graffiti
Onto empty buildings, tribute to her?

And **Gloriana** *is with her.*

We were confident. We knew she would save us.

Johanna *embraces her.*

Johanna   She sat amongst us, that first night.

Gloriana   Who are these people?

Johanna   Everyone. They have come from everywhere.
The boats, those ones from the centre, ones from the fire –

Gloriana   They were waiting for me?

Johanna   Yes.

Gloriana   How did they know?

Johanna   I told them.

Gloriana   Told them what?

Johanna   How you saved me. How you opened the gate,
took us out of fire –

Gloriana   I took you –

Johanna   – the gate was open and others followed –

Gloriana   – I did not know that.

Johanna   Others followed. And I told them you would
come to us.

Beat.

Johanna   Do you know how it is to be done?

How we are to stop the storm?

Gloriana   I am trying to learn.

Johanna (*to us*)   We call ourselves 'The Flood'. The ones out in the wilderness waiting. These sons and daughters of the storm. At first only I am close to her, but soon courage collects like coins in their pockets and they approach her, some shy watchful for miracles, others full of ideas –

Gloriana   – some of them want violence. They want to take back the city.

Johanna   – and what do you say?

Gloriana   What would it solve?

Johanna   They will do what you ask.

Gloriana   Who do you think I am?

Johanna   Sent from God.

Gloriana   That's what you told them?

Johanna   Yes.

Gloriana *moves away from her.*

Johanna (*to us*)   Each day she disappears into the wilderness. Her absences growing longer.

I tell 'The Flood' what little she knows of herself, what I know of her. These stories become currency, traded around the camp, embellished by every exchange. Altered. So that when they describe her it's a whole heartbeat until I recognise that girl that first came naked to the shore.

Each day new ones arriving –

Now **Sam**, *a hood pulled up around his face, joins her.*

Johanna   You have come to join us?

Sam   Yes.

Johanna   There is a place for you.

Sam   Is there?

Johanna   There's a building with a sheet for a roof. Out across the plain. We will bring food when we have it.

Sam   Where is she?

Johanna (*smiles*)   Out in the storm. But she will be here again.

Sam   Good.

Sam *leaves.*

Gloriana *now out in the Wilderness, under the rain and the storm.*

Sounds of the city/sounds of the storm.

Gloriana   I am lost
   Baffled
   It rains
   we don't know why.
   It rains we don't know who we are
   What is the storm?
   A thing of physics, a thing of the heart.
   The world's not dying it's killing itself.

(*looks up at the sky*) You know us don't you? You understand us.
   You know why I was put here, wonderfully made.
   The rain is glass upon which reflected
   We see our character. So speak to me!
   Every night I have sat here, every night silence.
   If I am unique am I responsible?
   I am here for a reason, am I not?
   Tell me how I can save them, save the world!

She puts her hands over her eyes.

Sounds of the city.

But no answer.

Gloriana   Nothing.

Now she starts to sing soft, supplicant to the skies.

Gloriana   Look up at the darkling sky above
  What can you see
  The stars they'll speak to you in beauty
  There's a smiling face looking down my love
  On you and me, on you and me –

Now **Kathryn** *walks out of the darkness.*

Gloriana *sees her.*

Kathryn *moves to her, kisses her, hands rough in her hair.*

After a moment **Kathryn** *steps back and slaps her, hard.*

They look at each other.

Kathryn   You left me behind.

Gloriana   Yes.

Kathryn   There's shelter?

Gloriana *holds out her hand.*

Johanna *outside the shell of a building in the Wilderness.*

Johanna (*to us*)   One night she did not return alone.

Kathryn *coming back through the Wilderness hand in hand
with* **Gloriana**.

Johanna   Who is this?

Gloriana   She is mine.

They stop poised on the threshold of a tent.

Gloriana (*to* **Kathryn**)   Come in with me.

Kathryn *enters.*

Gloriana (*smiles, to* **Johanna**)   Don't let anyone disturb me.

Gloriana *smiles again and enters the tent.*

Johanna (*to us*)   I sat guard that night.

Sam *appearing from the darkness.*

Sam   She is here?

Johanna   Inside.

Sam *edgy.*

Johanna   She is not alone.

Sam *loiters.*

Sam   Where you from?

Johanna   Iraq.

Sam (*a barely perceptible shift*)   You follow her?

Johanna   Yes.

Sam   Why?

Johanna   She saved my life.

Sam *listening.*

Sam   She's in there with a man?

Johanna   Perhaps.

(*to us*) Yes, I sat guard that entire night. Listened.

Her breath changing, rising above the rain, reaching for communion.

He was rapt, then shocked, then gone out into the night.

Sam *leaves.*

Johanna (*to us*)   Was *I* shocked? Yes.

Shocked like we should be sometimes: to a different sense of what is real.

She was flesh, was blood and bone; embodied: caught.

iv.vii

Now the **Captain** *and* **Natasha** *on a boat at sea, looking into the wilderness, rain coming down.*

Natasha   The wilderness is vast. How can we find anyone?

Captain   Turn off the light.

Natasha   What?

Captain   The torch.

She turns off the torch.

Captain   Look for other lights.

They scan the distant land.

Now **Natasha** *slips, tumbles down into the boat. He moves to her.*

Captain   Hurt?

Natasha   Just my pride.

She breathes in deeply. Looks up.

Natasha   Two old fools on a pleasure cruise.

She starts to laugh.

And then so does he. He leans his head back, rain pouring down.

Captain   Water on my face.

Worked in the Gulf of Mexico. We'd free dive, for fun I
mean, days off. No tanks, just a mask and you. Can train
yourself to go deeper, hold your breath for a lifetime. Your
head down, straight, past forty feet and then gravity flips
and the ocean sucks you in. Deeper. So deep you can't
possibly live but you do, because your body it remembers a
million years ago when you came out of the sea. It
understands that deep place; slows your heart, flattens your
lungs. And there's so much nitrogen in your blood, 150, 200,
250 feet you forget your own name, hallucinate, forget
you're beneath the sea: you swim into dreams. Some days I'd
do it again and again, past when it was safe. I'd do it again
and again because it was you I saw. You were my dream, in
the deep sea.

I know I am ruined. I know that.

I just wanted to say that to you, out loud.

She reaches out her hand to him. Silent moment.

Natasha   Look. Lights.

The lights of the encampment in the distance.

v.i

The encampment in the Wilderness.

Kathryn *emerging from the tent.*

Johanna *waiting for her.*

Johanna   You love her?

Kathryn   Yes.

Johanna   So do I. You came out for her? Are you here to take her from us?

Kathryn   No.

Johanna   She is responsible to all of us. Do you understand?

Kathryn   She's just the littlest thing. Remember that.

Gloriana *emerges from the tent.*

Gloriana   The fisherman is here.

Enter **Natasha** *and the* **Captain**, *exhausted.*

Natasha   My darling –

Natasha *moves to* **Kathryn**, **Kathryn** *moving away.*

Kathryn   Why are you here?

She takes her daughter's hands.

Natasha   For you.

Kathryn   You shouldn't have come.

Natasha   What's on your arm?

There is writing in Sharpie pen on her arm.

Kathryn My name.

Natasha Why?

Johanna If we die. People will know who we were. We all have it. Like in war.

Natasha Who is this?

Kathryn She follows the girl.

Johanna (*to* **Natasha**)   I know you, the powerful one. I have seen you on the television screen. Look. This is my name.

Johanna *raises her hands to her face. The letters of her name inked onto her fingers, practical homage to* **Gloriana**.

Natasha (*reads*)   'Johanna.'

Natasha *turns back to* **Kathryn**.

Natasha Come with me.

We have an hour.

Kathryn Why?

Natasha There's a helicopter coming. From the south.

Kathryn For you?

Natasha For us.

Kathryn You'd walk away?

Natasha I can't save them.

Kathryn She can.

Natasha Can you? Truly?

Johanna She can.

Natasha (*unsteady*)   Do you feel that?

The ground is shaking.

Kathryn   What?

Natasha   The ground. It's moving.

We have to leave this place.

Kathryn   I won't leave her.

Johanna   She will save us.

Natasha (*To* **Gloriana**.)   Do you know what to do child? Can you help us?

Sounds of the city, deafening.

Gloriana (*silent, shocked, shaking*)   I don't know.

Gloriana *runs away from them out into the Wilderness.*

Focus following her.

Gloriana   Listen!

Gloriana *held within the sounds of the city.*

Gloriana   I have listened but I haven't heard
I have witnessed but I have not seen
Somewhere within the maelstrom there must be –
Somewhere within the hate there must be –

Kathryn *following her,* **Gloriana** *seeing her now.*

Gloriana   Your face.

(*she smiles*) And I see it.

Epiphany.

The others joining now, **Natasha**, *the* **Captain**, **Johanna** –

Gloriana *looks up at the sky.*

Gloriana   I understand.

(*simply*) Stop.

The rain stops, dead.

Music out.

A thousand lights like slender individual pillars coming from the ground, unique, a widening circle around her, stretching out across the city, across the world.

Gloriana   – It is your face, you who I love, and her face she who loves you, and his face seeing her seeing you seeing me and it is a chain stretching ten thousand years and it is everywhere and endless –

She reaches out, mimes as if plucking one of the lights like a string.

Gloriana   Each voice a single strand in a single sentence in a vast conversation.

Individual voices rising now from the voices of the city.

As if she is plucking voices like violin strings.

Gloriana   Each voice a note in a song that is for ever.

Music back, rising.

Gloriana   – and it is connected we are connected each to each like every cell in every body, melded like each drop of water in the great sea –

We are *us*.

And that moment is Alleluia.

Johanna *has reached her.*

Johanna   You have stopped it –

Gloriana (*soft*)   No.

Johanna   – You have stopped the rain.

Gloriana   No one can stop the rain.

But we do not need to yield to it.

(*raising her voice vast to the whole plain*) This fragile moment. Do not forget it.

Johanna   You have saved us.

Gloriana   Just for one long breath.

Sam *is coming through the crowds of people, the* **Captain** *sees him first.*

Captain   No.

Natasha   What?

Captain   My son –

Rain returns, hard, beating down.

Natasha   What will he do?

Captain   The girl.

Johanna (*to us*)   And he was twenty feet from her now, ten, and she turns to him, her face wise and distant as a statue and she spreads out her arms soft, yielding –

Gloriana   Don't hurt him.

Kathryn   Why?

Gloriana   He's here to save his world.

Natasha   – Knife, he has a knife! –

Johanna   – (*to us*) Five feet, three –

And the **Captain** *launches himself at his son, crashes into him, sends him to the ground.* **Sam** *pushes him away, one punch, another, hits him with the butt of the knife, sends him staggering away. Turns to* **Gloriana.** **Kathryn** *rushing in to protect her now.*

Gloriana   Kathryn, no –

Sam *swinging the knife now,* **Kathryn** *stepping away.*

Sam *turning back to* **Gloriana.** *Approaching her, stalking prey. Now he raises the knife, sacrificial. Poised to strike. She does not shrink. And he stops. The knife dropping from his hands.*

Sam   Look.

Sam *gestures over her shoulder, out to sea.*

They turn to the sea.

Sam   A wave approaching –

Johanna   – A mile high –

Natasha   – A dozen miles across –

Johanna   – And Gloriana, exhausted, sank to her knees.

Rain back on, hard. **Sam** *runs away.*

Kathryn *is tottering now, moving unsteady. She puts her hand to her stomach. Raises it.*

Kathryn   Blood. (*looking for* **Natasha**) Mother? Mother –

Natasha *runs to her, catches her as she falls.*

Gloriana   The boat. We need to go to the boat.

v.ii

Projected huge, on wall: Again members of the community interviewed. Black backdrop, single camera, no interviewer visible or heard.

Underneath the sounds of the city, so for the first time we are going beyond simple documentary style with these projected inserts, they are become part of the dreamscape itself.

Woman A   We felt the ground shaking right across the city. I knew it was over then, knew something was coming for us now.

Man A   I saw the wave first, bedroom window, my wife trying to sleep. My daughter was away across the city, but the phones were down.

Woman B   The wave smashed through my windows and suddenly we were underwater. This isn't how I die I kept saying that. This isn't how I die.

Woman A   People were shouting 'Clear Out!' 'Clear Out!' Shouting in the street. But to where? Where could we have gone? We were the end of the line.

Man A   I would have liked that last phone call. My daughter. Terrible death is it, to drown? Terrible death.

Woman B   There was a man, alone, just down by the water. He saw the wave. Knew it was coming for him. But he didn't move. Just turned to face it. Passive. Silent.

– Cross fade this into main arena –

LX fast up on a different area of the City by the Sea, away from the House on the Hill, we see **Jack**. *He walks out into the open. He is carrying an Orange Migrants' lifejacket.*

The Wave approaching him. He standing without cover. He turns to face the wave.

v.iii

Music building.

Gloriana, **Kathryn** *and* **Natasha** *leaving the little boat, having reached an appropriate place in the City by the Sea. The* **Captain** *and* **Johanna** *still within the boat.*

Gloriana   Take the boat. Head up the coast. (*to* **Johanna**) Go with him! You must leave me now.

Natasha *pausing.*

Natasha   Matthew. Stay alive. I love you.

Captain   Yes.

Gloriana   Go!

Gloriana *carrying* **Kathryn**.

Natasha *following them.* **Natasha** *pauses, looks back out to sea. The wave vast now.*

Natasha   It's coming! Matthew, go! Go! Go!

The **Captain** *puts the throttle to full, the boat bombing away up the coast.*

The wave coming for them until they are lost to sight.

Gloriana   Come on! The highest point, that's where the helicopter will come. Follow me.

Gloriana *carries* **Kathryn** *up towards the House on the Hill.* **Natasha** *following, stumbling through the flood water.*

The Great Wave approaching. **Gloriana** *with* **Kathryn** *and* **Natasha** *stumbling into the House on the Hill and then up up up as high as they can go.*

As they move the projections return (or even just voice over if the voices are now established) –

Woman A   I saw so many taken, thousands taken by the Wave, their clothes ripped off.

Man A   torn naked by the savage power of the sea

Woman B   panic terror of letting go, of that first breath of water not air

Woman A   people saying singing crying out

Man A   every holy sentence they knew

Woman B   but the wave would not listen the wave did not care

Gloriana *and* **Natasha** *have reached the top of the House on the Hill by now. The wind howling.*

Gloriana *listening.*

Natasha   Can you hear it?

Listening, listening, listening. **Gloriana**. *Eyes closed.*

Gloriana *points, her head still down, marionette.*

Gloriana   There.

A helicopter searchlight, approaching.

RAF Pilot   – This is Raven Two Zero One Seven we have principal in sight –

Natasha *cradles* **Kathryn** *in her arms.*

Natasha   She's not breathing.

Natasha *places her hands on* **Kathryn**'s *stomach. Lifts them.*

Natasha   All this blood. Oh my child. She's not breathing.

Gloriana   Hold her. She knows it is her mother. Knows . . . It is you. (*Looks out over the city.*) The lights are going out now.

Across the city each of the thousand lights **Gloriana** *has lit going out fast, one by one.*

The waves crashes across the city now, destroying everything.

The land becoming sea.

Natasha *looks up at the sky. The wind howling.*

Natasha   They are here.

RAF Pilot   – This is Raven Two Zero One Seven we are attempting extraction standby –

The helicopter close now, its searchlight settling on them.

Gloriana   It is too close now.

Natasha   What do you mean?

Gloriana   The storm has them.

The wind too vicious. The helicopter searchlight out of control now, the helicopter trying to hold altitude and then spinning away.

RAF Pilot   – This is Raven Two Zero One Seven, cannot hold this, Mayday Mayday Mayday, going down hard Mayday Mayday Mayday –

The helicopter veers away from them.

Massive explosion as it crashes.

Natasha *cradling her daughter.*

Natasha   My daughter. O! O! O! What have you done?

I might have saved her. Listen, does she breathe?

Listens for breath.

If she lives everything's alright.

Gloriana   She is gone.

Natasha   You have allowed this? I thought you were

The baby. I thought you were an angel.

Natasha *sinks back on her heels, in shock.*

Gloriana *looks down onto the dead girl.*

Gloriana   The world is dark and descending and afraid.

I cannot hold the light. It is too much.

Gloriana *standing, looking out to sea.*

Gloriana (*to* **Natasha**)   Listen to me. We're going to
go down.

Go down to the deep place where there is peace.

Natasha   I can't leave her, I won't!

Gloriana   She has left us.

The wave vast above them now. **Gloriana** *grabs* **Natasha**, *holds
her tight.*

Gloriana   The wave's above, to live we dive below,

One breath in, deep, breath in, and now we go!

Gloriana *steps of the roof of the house falling into the water,*
Natasha *firm in her grasp.*

*The wave hits the House on the Hill, the highest point of the city and
it is engulfed.*

Now projection again: **Gloriana** *and* **Natasha** *under the water,* **Gloriana** *holding the older woman to her as the wave passes above them.*

Mirror image of **Gloriana** *from the Prologue, beneath the waves.*

And now the two women bursting to the surface again in real time, live on stage.

The great wave has passed.

The House on the Hill has disappeared.

Natasha *barely conscious.*

Gloriana *grabs a passing piece of wooden debris, levers the older woman onto it.*

Natasha *floating now on the wood, borne away from* **Gloriana** *by the current.*

Gloriana   Go now.

Natasha *lost from sight.*

The City by the Sea is vanished, replaced by the maelstrom.

The storm raging.

v.iv

Sounds of the city, fading.

Now **Gloriana***, standing alone on a piece of wood on the empty, burning sea.*

Gloriana   The world drowns where it doesn't burn, what to do?
    I'll not give up and neither should you,
    The world hates and it doesn't learn, what to do?
    I'll not give up and neither should you.
    Nothing now divides rich and poor,
    And all you loved seems taken away;
    Faith stirs solely within the empty soul'd,
    Hope lies naked prone on a torture table,
    Your dreams all drowned, compassions choked,
    Seems like all is passed away, all is gone,
    Alone on an empty sea, no land in view,
    The world needs to be made again, made anew:
    O yes, you're right to ask: what can we do?
    I'll not give up. My question is will you?

Gloriana *turns away from us and looks out to the water.*

She starts to paddle, a tiny figure on the wide sea.

Blackout.

Flood, Part III: To the Sea

A Play for Broadcast

Cast

In order of appearance

Sally	**Emma Bright**
Olivia	**Sally Ann Staunton**
Ingrid	**Joanna Nicks**
Jack	**Naveed Khan**
Zeina	**Yusra Warsama**
Gloriana	**Nadia Emam**
Sam	**Marc Graham**
The Captain	**Oliver Senton**
Kathryn	**Sarah Louise Davies**
Man In Car	**Tony Hind**

Survivors of the Flood

Jill Berry	Annie Holmes
Julie Blackie	Sirgius McHunu
Heather Cooper	Syeda Nudrat
Paul Dannatt	Allison Parker
Helena Gomes	Kevin Priestly
William Grunnil	

Creative Team

Director	Alan Lane
Designer	David Farley
Composer	Heather Fenoughty
Sound Designer	Matt Angove
Movement Director	Lucy Hind
Fight Director	Liam Evans-Ford
Associate Directors	Peter Bradley
	Sally Proctor
Design Assistant	Heledd Rees
Assistant Composer	Roma Yagnik
Lighting Technician	Adam Foley
Stage Managers	Calum Clark
	Olivia Dudley

Flymen	Elliot Gray
	Freddie Hall
Rain Operator	Madeleine O'Reilly
Pyrotechnics	Doug Nicholson of External Combustion
Set Construction	RT Scenic
Chef	George Allison
Project Dramaturg	Kara McKechnie
Digital Producer	Brett Chapman
Associate Producer	Sarah Cotterill
Producer	Joanna Resnick
Executive Producers	Mark Catley
	Laura Clark
	Jim Munro

For Archordia Strings

Cello	Lucy Revis
Violin/Viola	Paul O'Connor
Singer	Gina Walters

Recorded by James Fosberry at Bigdog Studios, Sheffield

Television Broadcast

Outside Broadcast	James Poole TV & Televideo
Technical Producer	James Poole
Unit Manager	James Mitchell
Sound	Sound Alliance
Camera Supervisor	Mike Callan
Cameras	Lincoln Abraham, Jon Dibley, Rob Sargent, Andre Seraille
Jib	Kevin French
Jib Assistant	Jack Davies
Camera Assistants	Alpha Barrie, Matthew Lightstone, Alex Rodin
Drone Operator	Chris Fenton
Vision Guarantee	Adam Robbins
Vision Engineer	Lewis Reed
RF Engineer	Andrew Woolhouse, David Crownshaw

Camera Guarantee	Alex Queen
Sound Guarantee	Simon Scrivener
VT Guarantee	Stefan Necula
Riggers	Nick Poole, Matt Limb
Generator	Film & TV Services, Nick Kennelly
Script Supervisor	Anna Charlton
Vision Mixer	Carol Abbott
Post Production	Storm HD
Offline Editor	James Bicknell
Online and Grade Editor	Paul Ingvarsson
Production Manager	Piera Buckland
Executive Producer For BBC	Emma Cahusac
Associate Producers For Arts Council England	Neil Darlison,Cassandra Mathers
Performance Live Strand Producers	Battersea Arts Centre, Andrew Fettis
Producer for Screen	Janie Valentine
Director for Screen	Ross MacGibbon

With thanks to . . . Henry Swindell.

Flood, Part Three: To the Sea was commissioned by Arts Council England, Battersea Arts Centre and the BBC as part of a series of programmes for BBC Arts called *Performance Live*.

The play was first broadcast on BBC Two in August 2017.

Filmed in June 2017 in Victoria Dock, Hull.

Characters

Three Girls, *survivors of the Wave.*
Gloriana, *a girl found in the depths of the sea.*
Zeina, *a survivor of the Wave.*
Jack, *an officer of the former migrant detention system.*
Kathryn, *a dead girl.*
Sam, *a survivor of the Wave.*
The Captain, *a survivor of the Wave.*

The crew and passengers of a fishing trawler.

Time: *After the Flood.*

Location: *The open sea and a single room on a makeshift island.*

NB. *This script is written for the televised broadcast of this play. As such it includes things which would not be included – and are not possible or relevant – if the play were to be presented solely as a piece of live theatre.*

i.i

Sound of children singing.

Empty water. The Flooded Land become sea.

Now a smartphone, floating in a waterproof cover.

It is not raining.

A hand reaching towards it, stretched out far, trying to grab it.

Misses, tries again, misses, finally grabs it.

Now we see three girls perched precariously on pieces of wood on the water, all connected, trying to stay level, trying not to fall in. The girl furthest out now holding the phone.

Sally (*whispers*)   Pull me in.

With great delicacy they start to pull her in, back to their larger platform.

Sally   Slowly slowly –

i.ii

A hand sorting through a filthy plastic box of wires, junk and paraphernalia. Takes a bodged iPhone charger with some new connectors.

Now connecting the iPhone charger to a car battery. Plugging in the phone. Practised hands.

The phone: charging icon.

Three girls clustered around the phone. Sally holding it. Excited.

Olivia   Turn it on.

Sally *turns it on.*

POV girls: Passcode screen.

Olivia   What's the code?

Ingrid   – How are we meant to know the code –

Olivia   Ssssh . . . We're not allowed in the battery room.

Sally *flips over the phone, looking for clues. The phone's wearing a happy multi-coloured case.*

Sally   I know the code.

Sally *punches in 1,2,3,4.*

The phone unlocks.

Ingrid   How did you know that?

Sally   Same as me. Me before.

Olivia   Got games?

Sally   Let's see who she was first.

Now flicking through phone apps. Finally: photos. We see photographs of a woman, Zeina, in happier times. Shopping, with a boyfriend, selfies, etc/ Sally flicking through. Now she pauses on a picture.

Close up of dirty hands, with letters tattooed into the fingers.

Olivia   Keep going.

Sally   No. Look.

Olivia   What is it?

Sally   The hands.

Ingrid   What about them?

Sally   The letters.

Ingrid   Tattoos.

Sally   They're her hands.

Olivia   Who?

Sally   *Her.* (*looking around her, nervous*) The girl. Look at the hands. G.l.o.r.i.a.n.a.

Ingrid   Gloriana. It is forbidden. To speak of her.

Olivia   I thought she was dead.

Beat. The freeze frame of those tattooed hands.

Then the girls deciding.

Olivia   I want to know.

Flicking through pictures.

Ingrid   Video. Play it.

Sally *presses play.*

Now rough-cut iPhone footage showing what we can of the Flood: not a little British local news affair but the real biblical deal.

Olivia   When the wave came –

Finger flicks to another video –

The wide free-flowing sea that used to be land. And in it, sticking up slanted, we see the very top of a pylon.

Sally   This is after.

Olivia   Play it.

Ingrid   Don't let anyone see.

The girls look back at the door. They decide. The girls watch the video.

i.iii

Now the crashing, grey sea. Rain, heavy.

A voice screaming.

Jack   Help! Help me!

*We see **Jack**, in the water.*

He is trying to swim away from a sinking electricity pylon, of which only the very top point is visible.

As the pylon sinks electrical sparks shower into the sea.

A woman, holding onto a piece of wood, across the waves from Jack.

Zeina   Swim away from the pylon! Swim towards me!

Jack   I can't. The current. Can't get away.

Zeina   I'll try and come for you.

Jack   Quickly, quickly –

Zeina *tries to swim towards him. More sparks from the pylon. It's clear the distance is too large to be bridged.*

Zeina   Swim to me! Come on!

Jack *is tiring.*

Jack   I can't. I can't –

Voice   Wait.

A figure balanced on a piece of wood, emerging from gloom.
Gloriana.

Gloriana   Take this.

She throws an orange life jacket, like those ones the migrants wear, attached to a thin rope. It lands near **Jack**.

Gloriana   Take it. Quickly!

Jack, *exhausted, tries to grab the life jacket. Misses, tries again, grabs it. Holds it now.*

Sparks again, as the pylon sinks closer.

Gloriana   I'm going to pull you out.

Gloriana *jumps down into the water, uses the wooden platform to balance the rope and begins to pull him away from danger. The pylon lowering.*

Jack   Quickly! Please! Quickly!

Zeina   Swim, man, help her!

The pylon sinks into the water. Massive explosion of sparks, engulfing that section of water.

Gloriana *pulls again on the rope.*

Jack *emerges from the smoke, alive.*

Slowly she pulls him towards her. **Jack** *spluttering, broken, taking in water.*

Zeina *swimming to her now too.*

Finally, the three converge. Resting against the wooden detritus. **Jack** *silent.*

Zeina   Is he dead?

Gloriana   No.

Zeina   We won't survive out here.

Gloriana *silent, watching the girl.*

They look out across the waves.

Zeina   It's over isn't it?

Gloriana   What?

Zeina   England.

Jack *splutters to life, spits out sea water. He looks across at the women. His eyes focusing now on* **Gloriana.**

Jack   You.

Gloriana   Yes.

Now suddenly bubbles coming from the water beneath them. **Zeina** *panicking.*

Zeina   What is it? What's happening?

Jack   I don't know.

Zeina   Shark?

Gloriana   No shark.

A bang from underwater, and now an object surfacing from beneath the waves.

A caravan, now bobbing uncertainly at the surface.

Gloriana   Come on.

They swim to the caravan and struggle on board. **Zeina** *helping* **Jack,** **Gloriana** *the last to lift herself on board.*

Zeina   Will it hold us?

Gloriana   Balance it.

Now a frantic balancing act: a dumb show in which all three stand on the floating caravan and struggle to keep it both level and floating.

Eventually they find themselves standing apart but balanced, the caravan not sinking.

They sit, tentative, shivering, exhausted.

ii.i

The three girls watching the video on the phone.

Now footsteps in the corridor outside the door, the girls terrified, moving quickly, hiding the phone.

Door being pushed open. A shadow intruding. **Sam**.

Sam   What are you doing in here?

Sally   Making the memory poem. Like you said. So we can pass on what happened.

Sam   And?

Looks across to the other girls.

Olivia   What was it like, life after the wave?

Ingrid   Like you woke up from a little sleep.

Sally   And your Ma, she's forgot she's your ma.

Olivia   Don't know your face –'

Beat.

Ingrid   'What was it like, life after the wave?

Olivia   We knew we must build a new world.

Sally   We knew we must harden our hearts.

Ingrid   Cause all was lost' –

Sam   – Good. Good.

He leaves. They wait, eyes flicking to each other, deciding.

Sally   Get the phone again.

They reach for the concealed phone.

ii.ii

The floating caravan.

Gloriana, **Zeina** *and* **Jack** *sitting at different corners of the floating caravan.* **Jack** *looking down at the edge.*

Gloriana   The current's taking us further out.

Jack   Are we lower? Are we sinking?

Gloriana   Not yet.

Jack   We're too heavy.

Zeina   It'll float.

Jack   For how long?

Gloriana   Long enough.

Zeina *has her phone out and is recording video of the sea.*

She looks back at **Jack**. *From deep in his pockets he pulls out a tube of mints. Looks at them, looks at her. Offers her one.*

Zeina   Thank you.

Jack (*gestures the phone*)   What are you doing?

Zeina   People should know what happened here.

Jack   What people? What happened here happened everywhere. You think there's a light in the sky coming to help us? Think there's a white ship approaching?

Zeina   Don't know.

Jack (*indicating* **Gloriana**)   She might.

Zeina   You know each other?

Jack   Oh, you know who she is.

Zeina   I don't.

Jack   Look at her hands.

Zeina   What do you mean?

Jack   Look.

Zeina *hesitates then scrambles, unsteady, near to* **Gloriana**.

Zeina   What does he mean?

Gloriana *resistant for a long moment, then exposes her hands. First by her sides, and as* **Zeina** *still has her camera phone running we see letters tattooed into them. And then* **Gloriana** *yields, raises her hands to her face. The letters spelling out a name:* **Gloriana**.

The same freeze frame the girls saw in the first scene: her hands, tattooed.

Zeina   The girl from the sea.

Jack   Yeah.

Zeina   You're real.

Jack   You do know her.

Zeina *looks at* **Gloriana**.

Zeina   I know what they said. The girl from the sea.
    She came to us one dawn, they say. Far out

One dawn alone beneath the wine dark sea.
Fishermen hauling up nets from deep water
From seventy metres down in the dark
They pulled up one net empty of all fish.
In it one hundred lifejackets
Orange like those migrants left on beaches.
Once. Like those we wear now, we survivors.
One hundred life jackets and a girl.
Curled pale naked just bandages on hands
A drownded girl. Her name tattooed.
And she sat up. Alive. It was you, was it?

Beat.

Gloriana   Yes.

Zeina   And then, straight after, the rain. Then the wave.

Was it because of you? All this? The rain?

Gloriana   I don't know.

The three have become drawn deep into their conversation, the outside world ignored.

Now a big bang on the side of the floating caravan.

The caravan lurches. Shock. The three occupants afraid.

Zeina   What is it?

They scramble to see, scared. A body, floating in the water, which has crashed into the caravan and floated a little distance away. Uniform of a Coast Guard.

Gloriana   Life Saver. Drownded.

The body moving closer.

Gloriana   Come on.

She stands, edges towards the limits of the caravan.

Jack   He's dead, what are you going to do, bury him?

Gloriana   He'll have stuff we need. Come on.

They form a human chain to balance the caravan and reach out, Jack reluctantly joining in. Eventually **Gloriana***, at the extreme end of the chain, grasps the body.*

Gloriana   There's a whistle around his neck.

Gloriana *slipping into the water pulls the whistle from the corpse, puts her hands into the pockets, finds a knife in the belt. She pulls it free.*

Gloriana   Knife.

Throws the knife back to the caravan, where **Jack** *takes it. Now* **Gloriana** *pulls a Marine Flare from the body, tosses it up onto the caravan.*

Zeina   What's that?

Gloriana   Flare.

Gloriana *pulls herself back onto the caravan. It lurches as she gets back 'onboard', unsteady.*

Jack   Cold.

Gloriana   Put the jacket on. Extra layer.

Jack *hesitates and then puts on the orange life jacket, reluctant.*

Zeina (*to* **Jack**)   You know her?

Jack   Yeah.

Zeina   How?

Gloriana   The detention centre they took me to.

Zeina (*to* **Jack**)   You were an illegal?

Gloriana   He was in charge.

Camera lingers on the shivering man in his new orange life jacket.

Gloriana   Look!

Zeina   What is it?

Gloriana   Car.

A car, submerged within the water is floating towards the caravan.

Zeina   It's sinking.

Gloriana   Quiet. Listen.

Silence. Now they hear a repeated thud coming from the car.

Zeina   There's someone in there.

Gloriana *slips from the caravan into the water, swims to the car. Pounds on the boot, unable to open it.* **Zeina** *swims out a few feet from the caravan, stops, afraid.* **Jack** *remains on the caravan.*

Gloriana   I need something to break the glass. Jack! The knife. Jack!

Jack   We can only float with three. You know that.

Jack *turns away.*

Gloriana *pounds harder on the boot of the car. An answering thump from within, weakening now.*

Zeina   They're drowning.

The thumps quietening to silence now.

Gloriana *gives up, rests her head against the car, listens.*

Gloriana   Going now.

The car sinking from sight.

Gloriana *swims back to the caravan, lets the car go.*

She attacks **Jack***, beats the shit out of him, is a heartbeat from tearing out his throat with her teeth.*

The caravan lurches, starts to sink with their motion.

Zeina   Stop it, we'll sink! Stop!

Silence, the sound of their breathing.

Gloriana *grabs the knife from* **Jack** *and retreats, an angry lioness.*

Zeina   We'll die here, won't we?

iii.i

The room.

The three girls lie on the floor, sharing the single screen of the phone, watching rapt.

As if they were kids before the cataclysm, watching videos online.

iii.ii

The floating caravan.

The rain sheeting down now.

Gloriana, **Jack** *and* **Zeina** *huddled together: frozen, hungry, exhausted.*

Jack   It'll be the cold, not the water.

Zeina   What?

Jack   That kills us.

Silence.

Zeina   Did you see any jumpers?

Not jumpers, that's wrong. Divers. Drowners.

But I mean like that day when the planes went into the towers and those people they were caught *above* the fire. No escape, no help coming, just deciding when to go. Jumpers.

I saw a couple, man and woman, not long after the wave, when everything had become sea. On a little bit of wood. Water rising. And you could see them, see the decision. And they stepped off. Into deep water. And held each other down. They held hands you see, when they jumped, so they could hold each other down. Did she change her mind, did he hold her? That's what I wondered, but no I think they were together –

One minute, two. All done.

They'd decided: no more of this. No more.

Like the jumpers, when the planes came out of the blue sky.

Jack   I'm not jumping.

Zeina   You sure of that?

Jack   It doesn't mean anything if it ends like this. Doesn't mean anything.

Zeina   What?

Jack   Everything that came before. The world. That it was ordered.

Zeina   And you think it did?

Jack   Yes. (*Passionate.*) Yes, it did.

Gloriana *stands. She's heard something before she's seen it. Head to one side, eyes closed, an animal scenting danger.* **Zeina** *follows her gaze.*

Zeina   What?

Gloriana (*she opens her eyes*)   There.

Jack   A boat.

A fishing trawler appearing out of the gloom.

Jack   It's one of the trawlers. That took people from the wreckage of the city.

Zeina   Took people?

Jack   For money. For whatever they could trade. To find a new place.

Jack *puts the whistle to his lips, blows.*

The trawler coming close to them, oblivious. The trawler crammed full of people, piled on top of each other, each wearing an orange life jacket. Shattered, stinking people, minds lost. Silent, sealed within their own separate worlds.

Jack *and* **Zeina** *move to the side of the caravan closest to the approaching boat, background.*

Gloriana *steps into the foreground, corner of the caravan, speaks directly to us.*

And at the end of the speech we move to **Jack** *as he tries to board the boat –*

Gloriana   They wore each others piss and tears, life jackets
Orange like those the migrants left on beaches
Once, when chaos was far away and there was order
And England was England, and exile elsewhere.
Now they live two-headed, one faced forward one back;
Backwards face wearing a narcotic smile
Dreaming vivid through the palace of their past.
The forward face, that sees now not then: blank.
They're silent, shocked, cause this should not be them.
These now homeless minds, that don't know themselves:
Cause who we are seems link'd to where we are.
Silence, until Jack comes scrabbling up the side
And one turns, says –

Migrant   There's no room on the boat.

Gloriana   The rain falling.

Migrant   There's no room on the boat.

Jack *angry, trying to force his way over the side of the boat.*

He turns back to **Gloriana** *and* **Zeina**.

Jack   Come on! We can live.

Zeina *moves towards him, tentative. Looks back to* **Gloriana**.

Gloriana *shakes her head.*

Jack *has clambered onto the side of the trawler, now more in than out.*

Migrant   There's no room for you all.

Jack *looks back down at* **Zeina** *and* **Gloriana**. *Decides. Turns back to the boat people.*

Jack   Take one. Take me. Forget them.

Zeina   No!

Jack *steps forward onto the boat.*

Migrant   There's no room for one.

Jack   What do you mean?

There's always room for one.

I have money, here. It's in a pouch, waterproof.

He scrabbles beneath clothes.

I can't find it. I can't –

Please.

I am English too.

This is the hardest test of my life.

I was powerful before. I had a serious job and people they listened to me –

Migrant   There's no room for one.

But **Jack** *is beyond reason now. He pushes forward, struggling to get on board the boat.*

Now a migrant stands, pushes him back. **Jack** *pushes forward again. The migrant hits him, hard.* **Jack** *falls back, stands again, and pushes forward, determined.*

Zeina (*to* **Gloriana**)   Help him.

Jack *stands again, and now the migrants rise up as one against him. One by one the passengers of the boat shaken to consciousness and united in violence against* **Jack**. *They rain blows down on him, beating him to the ground, keep hitting him even as he lies prone. A beating becoming a lynching.*

Gloriana *reaches the edge of the caravan, where it meets the boat now. Looks up into the melee. People pelting* **Jack** *with blows, all the rage of their terrible situation unleashed.*

And in the crowd **Gloriana** *sees the* **Captain***, and he sees her.*

They are two still points in the moving scene.

The **Captain** *raises his hand, silent recognition. He does not move to stop the fight.*

Final blows are now being rained down on the motionless body of **Jack***.*

Zeina (*to* **Gloriana**)   Can't you stop this?

The knife in **Gloriana***'s hands, the marine flare.*

Gloriana (*decides*)   No.

Zeina   They'll kill him.

Gloriana   Yes.

She turns away.

Eventually **Jack***'s body is pushed over the side into the water.*

The boat continues its journey.

The two women watch it disappear into mist.

– Time passing –

iv.i

The floating caravan.

Gloriana *and* **Zeina** *huddled in the centre of the roof.*

Zeina   Water's rising.

Gloriana   Yes.

Zeina *sits up, looks out.*

Zeina   Nothing.

Gloriana   The current, it's taken us out to sea. Deep
water now.

Zeina   No one's coming are they?

Are you afraid?

Gloriana   No.

Beat.

Zeina   My parents, I saw them die. But they were together.

Beat.

Zeina   Was there someone, that you loved?

Gloriana   Yes.

Zeina   Gone?

Gloriana   Yes.

Zeina   Who was it?

Gloriana   She was . . . Fierce. And lost. She made me laugh.
I did not know her long enough.

Zeina *reaches out her hand to* **Gloriana**. *The tattooed fingers now
concealed by another's hands. Now she pulls her close.* **Gloriana**
yields. Two women curled together on a dwindling platform.

Zeina   Water's rising.

Gloriana   Don't move. Gentle.

Beat.

Gloriana   I remember the sounds of the sea. The whales,
they sing across oceans. I would dream of them, sometimes,
I think.

Gloriana *curls herself on the rooftop. Exhausted.*

Zeina   The planes, they came out of the blue sky. And the
people in the buildings, they never knew why the world
ended.

Zeina *looks across to* **Gloriana**, *who has finally succumbed to a sort of sleep.*

The water rising on the caravan.

Zeina *sits up. She decides.*

She takes off her orange life jacket. Lays it gently on top of the sinking caravan.

Now she takes her phone from her zipped pocket.

Turns on the video recorder, speaks softly to it.

Zeina   My name was Zeina Allan. My father was Richard. My mother was Amal. They were taken by the wave. I was a citizen of England. I did not think I would be a jumper. I want you to know that I tried. I tried my hardest for as long as I could.

She puts the phone inside the waterproof holder we recognise from the beginning of the story. She leans out over the water, and places the phone on the surface. She pushes it away out onto the sea, a modern message in a bottle.

Now she looks back at **Gloriana**.

Zeina   Good luck.

She turns back to the water. She steps off the caravan. The cold water shocking, causing her to gasp.

Whilst she still has strength she swims away from the caravan, a tiny head on the wide sea, gone now.

iv.ii

Now with the girls crouched around the phone.

Ingrid   What happened? What did she do?

Sally   She gave up. She gave in to the sea.

Now back to **Gloriana**, *who wakes. Looks around the sinking caravan, sees that it is empty, understands.*

Gloriana   No. No. No!

Her rage and despair coming. Punching the metal roof of the caravan, screaming out her anger. Animal.

The caravan lurching with her motions, the water higher again, the vehicle more precarious.

Olivia   She left Gloriana alone.

Gloriana *looking out onto the vast sea. Closes her eyes. Deciding. Music building –*

Ingrid   No one survives alone, out there.

Olivia   The sea, it goes into you, makes you mad.

Sally   Gloriana. *She* would not give in. She would not step off –

And now **Gloriana** *steps off the caravan, onto the sea.*

And walks on water.

She walks out into darkness. **Gloriana** *walking out onto the sea, now reaching a square of dark water, lit by fire.*

Sally   Where could she go?

Ingrid   Where would we go, if we could?

Olivia (*simple*)   We would go home.

Ingrid   Where? There is no home, now –

Gloriana *pauses.*

In the centre space, torches around her.

She sees **Kathryn**, *beautiful dress flowing.*

Kathryn   Here.

Gloriana   This is home?

Kathryn   Yes.

Gloriana   Where is it?

Kathryn   Where doesn't matter. You think home is a place.
It's not. It is –

Gloriana (*understanding*)   – a once, it is a one time, a
moment, when there was peace –

Kathryn   it is you, it is me.

Kathryn *smiles.*

Now they dance in the fire-drawn square. **Gloriana** *caked in dirt,*
Kathryn *perfect.*

We hear the love theme –

Song   Look across the ocean of our love
   What do you see
   A new world one where we will be free
   We'll sail across that ocean, oh my love
   Just you and me, just you and me

   Look up at the darkling sky above
   What can you see
   The stars they'll speak to you in beauty
   There's a smiling face looking down O my love
   On you and me, on you and me

   Take my hand and dive beneath the waves
   What will we see
   Deep inside the heart of our mystery
   And you know together we'll be saved
   O you and me, O you and me

The dance ending.

Gloriana   – O you and me –

Kathryn   You're tired to the bone aren't you?

Gloriana   Yes.

(*Crumbling like a little girl.*) I couldn't save you.

I think you were the one I was meant to save.

Kathryn   No.

Gloriana   That was the whole point of me

Kathryn   Doesn't look like it.

Gloriana   Where are we? Is this where the dead go?

Kathryn   Just night, on the sea.

Gloriana   I can't go on.

Kathryn   You will.

Gloriana   I can't go on.

Kathryn (*grabs her viciously*)   You will, you fucking will –

Gloriana (*pushing herself away*)   Why?

Kathryn   For me. For all the lost ones. Just because the world did not support what you believed it doesn't mean what you believed is wrong.

Gloriana   How will I?

Kathryn   Look at me
Look at me
Win.

Gloriana   Everything is lost.

Kathryn   Not yet.

Kathryn *turns away and walks out onto the dark sea, away.*

Kathryn   I'll always be here. This will always be here.

(*Sings soft.*) And if we're ever forced oceans apart
Where might you be
I'll skim a stone across the wild sea
And you'll know that you still hold my heart
Cause I am you, and you are me

Kathryn *is gone.*

Gloriana *alone on the wide dark sea.*

v.i

Now the girls re-watching **Zeina**'s *last message. Sound via the phone –*

Zeina 'I was a citizen of England. I want you to know that I tried. I tried my hardest for as long as I could . . .'

And now the shadow approaching the door again.

Sally He's coming he's coming he's coming.

Olivia Stop it.

They press pause. Afraid. They hide the phone.

Shadow pausing outside the door. **Sam**.

Girls looking to each other: come on, do something.

Ingrid 'What was it like, life after the wave

Olivia We knew we must build a new world

Sally We must be strong, must forget pity

Ingrid And force will win all –'

The shadow leaves.

Olivia We can't keep the phone. If he finds it he'll drown us, like he did the other ones.

Ingrid What do we do?

Sally *takes the phone.*

She turns on the video, and speaks into it.

Sally My name is Sally. I survived the wave. I've not given up. Watch the videos on this phone. You'll understand why. *She* lives.

Now **Sally** *places the phone back into its protective cover. The girls stretch themselves out onto the water, reverse of the image from the first scene of this play. They send the mobile phone out onto the waters.*

Sally   Pull me in.

Sally *steps back onto the platform –*

Ingrid   You believe Gloriana is still out there?

They look out to sea.

Olivia   How could she have survived?

Sally   – She did.

Ingrid   Why?

Sally   Because it is necessary.

v.ii

Now we find **Gloriana** *again, lying on top of the caravan once more.*

The water higher again, approaching her prone body, closing in. Filthy, bloodstained Ophelia. The caravan ready to sink. Exhausted like a dream.

She looks out across the sea.

Whale spouts, close to the caravan.

Whale song in the sound.

She smiles, weakly. Her head slipping back.

More spouts.

In the makeshift room the girls sit in a circle. Concentrating.

Then **Sally** *begins, an improvised poem.*

The girls all trying to pick it up and make it up as they go on, the lines being repeated underneath, a type of call and response, the making of a new improvised history.

Sally   'She'll come to us one dawn. The girl

Olivia   Her name carved deep in her hands

Ingrid   The girl from the sea, Gloriana –

Sally   And what must be will be.'

Now on the caravan **Gloriana** *lifts her head a final time.*

Music building –

Gloriana *forcing herself from her shattered sleep, the water over her ankles now.*

Eyes hollowed out, the ends of her endurance. Lifting herself to her feet.

Ingrid   'She'll come to us one dawn. The girl.

Olivia   She'll come and she'll know what to do

Sally   The sea will teach her our way home

Ingrid   And what must be will be –'

Gloriana *looking out over the vast empty sea. Standing, swaying. Listening.*

Now she stands utterly still.

There's a light in the sky, approaching.

She smiles.

She pulls the flare from her tattered coat. Lights it.

The light in the sky seemingly disappeared. The caravan sinking completely beneath the waves.

Gloriana *closes her eyes.*

Olivia   'She'll come to us one dawn. The girl

Sally   Safe, free, wise from her night journey

Ingrid   The girl who saves, the promised one

Olivia   And what must be will be' –

The beam of light returning. Settling on **Gloriana***. The light on her blinding. She looks up into it. Opens her eyes.*

Blackout.

Flood, Part IV: New World

A Play

Cast

In order of appearance

Natasha	**Lisa Howard**
Johanna	**Rani Moorthy**
Sam	**Marc Graham**
Ingrid	**Joanna Nicks**
Sally	**Emma Bright**
Olivia	**Sally Ann Staunton**
Gloriana	**Nadia Emam**
The Captain	**Oliver Senton**
Man A	**Dave Pattison**
Woman A	**Louise Brown**
Woman B	**Polly Pattison**
Bus Driver	**Ash Schultz**

Inhabitants of the Three Islands

Caroline Blair	John Hinson
Ean Blair	Ced Illidge
Hannah Brace	Andrew Kenny
Lesley Brown	Dave Miller
Vicki Brownlee	Nigel D. Morpeth
Katherine Carter	Yvonne Oliver
Joanna Dunn	Julie Robinson
Janice Edmonds	Ash Schultz
Martyna Harasimiuk	Roy S Settle
Abbey Headland	

Creative Team

Director	Alan Lane
Designer	David Farley
Composer	Heather Fenoughty
Sound Designer	Matt Angove
Lighting Designer	Katharine Williams
Movement Director	Lucy Hind
Fight Director	Liam Evans-Ford

Associate Directors	Ingrid Adler
	Peter Bradley
	Sally Proctor
Design Assistant	Heledd Rees
Chief LX	Alex Johnston
Stage Managers	Calum Clark
	Olivia Dudley
	Elliot Gray
	Freddie Hall
	Marek Streit
Boat Crew	Hamish Ellis
Pyrotechnics	Doug Nicholson of External Combustion
Set Construction	RT Scenic
Chef	George Allison
Project Dramaturg	Kara McKechnie
Digital Producer	Brett Chapman
Associate Producer	Sarah Cotterill
Producer	Joanna Resnick
Executive Producers	Laura Clark
	Jim Munro

Flood, Part Four: New World was commissioned by Hull UK City of Culture 2017.

The play will be first performed on 26 September 2017 in Victoria Dock, Hull.

Part Four is being published before rehearsals commence, so certain alterations may occur prior to performance.

Characters

Gloriana, *a girl found in the deeps of the sea, now missing.*
Natasha, *the former Minister for Overseas, now the leader of Renaissance Island.*
Johanna, *an Iraqi Christian, now the leader of the Holy Island.*
Sam, *a former fisherman, now the leader of Albion Island.*
The Captain, *a former fisherman, now resident of the Holy Island.*
Sally, *A resident of Albion Island.*
Olivia, *A resident of Albion Island.*
Ingrid, *A resident of Albion Island.*
Various inhabitants of the Three Islands

Location: *Three makeshift islands becoming City States, and the empty sea.*

'Even in our sleep, pain which cannot forget falls drop by drop upon the heart until, in our own despair, against our will, comes wisdom through the awful grace of God.'

Robert Kennedy, slightly misremembering Aeschylus, in a speech announcing the assassination of Martin Luther King, 1968.

i.i

Three makeshift islands alone on the empty, wild sea. Perhaps the remnants of the very highest ground, or just platforms and metal lashed together. A home that is a life raft. On them the shattered survivors of the Wave. The islands littered with detritus, with fragments of the society that once went before.

And now we see the islanders begin to build structures on the islands, see them to try to form order from chaos, see them make the beginnings of their new societies.

And as they build we build a song. Starting just with one or two, then growing and growing until by the end each survivor is singing. Three communities being built as three makeshift islands of shelter rise from the waves.

i.ii

Projected: The Faces we recognise from Part Two. Same background.

Island Construction continues under this to buy more time and get a double visual –

Man A   What was it like? After the wave? Everything was gone. The land was sea. It was luck, where you ended up. If you ended up, or just ended –

Woman A   We hung onto bits of wood, anything, looked for little boats, looked for help. Corpses floating on the water. I was on the water three days, alone, bit of wood, before a boat found me. I thought I was dead before they found me, thought this is hell –

Woman B   – Worst days of all were the days straight after the wave. Most of the people who died they actually died in the days after. And most people did die. They drowned, starved. Died of thirst. Died of each other too: people killed to live, killed out of fear, it was savage –

Man A   – you need to understand, England was gone. I don't just mean the soil, the land, I mean the whole thing. Idea of it. We were left alone: had to start again, from what we knew, from what we were –

Woman A   – Man and a woman in a boat, little rubber boat, found me. Torch light in the night. Three days. Thought it was God come for me. He was busy I thought, it took him that long to find me –

Woman B   – we started again. Wasn't really an island, was a platform bolted together, just above water line. Growing day by day. Didn't know if there were others. We had to make up how we were going to live, what the law was, who was to blame, who was to lead. You start again, don't you, you do what you have to –

Man A   – And then, one day the rain stopped.

Rain out on islands. Inhabitants coming out of any shelters, looking up to sky.

Man A   And we looked out on a new world. Sky dark and grey, like a nuclear winter. The sun just a remembered promise, an uncertain shadow, invisible above endless clouds. We lived, all the months that followed, somewhere between night and day, struggling to believe in dawn. And all of us, everyone, at the back of our minds had one question: What if the wave returns?

– Time passing –

i.iii

Now focus to **Natasha**, *who stands alone on the edge of Renaissance Island, looking out to sea.*

Natasha *talks to us.*

Natasha   Always and again it comes to the city.
      To how we might live, together, or not.
      Can we build back better than we had before?

Scowling once she said to me, my daughter
My darling one, she said: 'You have failed us.'
Perhaps I did. All of you, my children.
You know what price I paid. The price was her.
My child bleeding out in my helpless arms,
My child trafficked away into night. All gone.
O Kathryn, O my child.
Grief's not sorrow for what the lost one lost,
Their own life stolen away, their future past,
It's more; it's rage at what was taken from you.
She was mine, she was my world without end
My answer to this insoluble life.
Her killers: What price should they pay?
There is hate in me, second beat of my heart.
My mind knows what you know, knows that violence
Is a circle, a snake swallowing its tail,
But my heart it is savage for vengeance –

Enter **Man A**.

Man A   – They need you now.

Natasha   I know. (**Man A** *stands apart.* **Natasha** *talks to us.*)
Once again I lead.
My little one when little she loved the penguins
Watched them rapt on the BBC, called out –
'Mummy, mummy, they cuddle against the wind!'
We're like that now, penguin huddled, arctic storm;
Stunned silent, solely seeking survival.
But when the wind relents, what rage will come?
There will be blame yes, but should there be blood?

Natasha *turns and walks towards the massing people of her island.*

Man A   What are we to do?

Resident   How are we to continue?

Natasha (*raising her voice*)   We are to keep separate. We are
to make things as they were before.

– Time passing –

i.iv

Now focus shifts to **Johanna**, *alone at the edge of Holy Island.*

She talks to us.

Johanna   What is the power of faith? What can it alter?
　　Gloriana was sent to save the world
　　　This is what I believe.
　　　Yet the world is sunk and burning and afraid
　　　Gloriana was sent to save the world
　　　Yet she is disappeared, shrunk to rumour
　　　And now we who loved her are shipwrecked,
　　　Trafficked, cast adrift on the wild sea.
　　　She's lost but I feel the meaning of her
　　　Here, in my heart's mind, where absolute truth lies.
　　　I see her now, face moving on the waters.
　　　If we lose you then we will lose ourselves.

Gloriana*'s face, huge on the water.*

　　They will say you mean nothing, that your name
　　Is failure, is fraud. Gloriana.
　　The girl from the sea, sent to save us all.
　　What if your purpose was shrouded, hidden?
　　What if the truth was you were more than you?
　　If the truth is what you did is less important
　　Than what you meant? Gloriana.

Enter **Woman A**, *orange life jacket from the wilderness. Others joining.*

Woman A   Teacher, what we will do now?

Johanna   We will pray.

Woman A   For what?

Resident   To who?

Johanna   To her. Gloriana.

Woman A   But she has disappeared,

Resident   Abandoned us,

Woman A   She did not stop the wave,

Resident   She lied to us –

Johanna *turns back to them. Rapt.*

Johanna   No! I have seen a vision of beauty

Seen a great light flashing from the deep sea –

Resident   Where is she?

Johanna   She is within us, always.

The crowds gathering around her, listening.

Johanna   Yes, I have seen a vision of great hope –

– Time passing –

i.v

Now to **Sam***, alone on the shore of Albion Island. His hands over his eyes, now withdrawing them, looking out to sea. He talks to us.*

Sam   Whenever I close my eyes I see the knife.
　　My arm extended, bright blade reaching out,
　　Her little face, beneath, somehow accepting;
　　Those eyes a dark sky full of stars glittering
　　Then in them reflected the wave above
　　Pitiless, slab sided like a canyon
　　Arcing over me: a mile high, mile across.
　　I did not strike down, I did not end it then.
　　That was the moment. But I was afraid.
　　What is the cost of fear, of weakness?

Now he calls over his shoulder.

Sam   All of you, bring him here to me and listen.

Enter the residents of Albion Island.

Amongst the crowd **Sally***,* **Olivia** *and* **Ingrid***.*

In the centre of the group a man, afraid, pushed towards **Sam***. The crowd forming around them both.* **Sam** *confronts the man. A coiled, animal energy in* **Sam***.*

Sam   Do you deny that I lead here?

Man   No.

Sam *punches him in the stomach. The man folds over.* **Sam** *stepping back and looking to the crowd.*

Sam   What are the laws here? What is our history?

Sam *hunting the faces for answer. Eyes settle on* **Ingrid**.

Ingrid   Our history?

Sally (*trying to help the other girl*)   He means the memory poems –

Ingrid (*panicking under* **Sam**'*s gaze*)   I –

Olivia (*sotto voce*)   You know –

Sally (*picking up*)   'What was it like, life after the wave? –'

Ingrid (*afraid and trying to remember takes the cue*)   'What was it like, life after the wave?'

Sally   'We knew we must build a new world'

Ingrid (*still stumbling, echoing and struggling to keep up through the below*)   'We knew we must build a new world'

Olivia (*joining*)   'We knew we must harden our hearts.'

Sally   'What was it like, life after the wave?'

Olivia   'Like you woke up from a little sleep'

Sally   'And your ma, she's forgot she's your ma'

Olivia   'And she don't even know your face –'

Sally   'What was it like, life after the wave?'

Sam (*over them as they continue*)   What's the law?

Sally   'We knew who brought the storm, the rain'

Olivia   'We knew it was the girl to blame'

Sally   'And any who speak of her must die'

Ingrid (*certain now, louder*)   'And any who speak of her must die.'

Beat. The man has got to his feet.

Sam   This was found, hidden near where you sleep.

Sam *flourishes a piece of paper.*

Olivia   What is it?

Ingrid   What's written there?

Sally   – It's a drawing of a fish, like children would draw –

Olivia   – That's her symbol –

Ingrid   – Like those things written on her body, they say –

Man   I did not do this.

Sam *approaches the* **Man**.

Sam   Who rules here?

Man   You do.

Sam   Do you want to challenge me?

Man   No.

Sam *hits the* **Man** *again, and again. The* **Man** *collapses.*

Sam   This is yours, yes?

The **Man** *dragging himself to his feet again, silent.*

Sam   Is it just you, or are there others?

Man   I didn't do this.

Sam   It was found close to where you sleep.

Sam *hits him again, knocks him to his knees.*

Sam   Do you want to challenge me?

Man *swaying, sobbing, on his knees.*

Man   No.

Sam   Are there others?

Man   No.

Sam   Tomorrow: the water.

Man   No!

Sam (*to others in the crowd*)   Take him away.

You all know who rules here and why.

Do you want it to return? Do you want the wave to come back?

*The **Man** is escorted away.*

Sam *and other residents leave.* **Sally**, **Olivia** *and* **Ingrid** *remaining by the sea shore.*

Sally   Do you know that man?

Olivia   He sleeps two shelters down from us –

Sally   – From before I mean –

Olivia   My cousin knew him I think. He drove a bus –

Sally   – Your cousin?

Olivia   – yes.

Sally   Is he weak?

Olivia   Weak?

Sally   Can he be trusted –

Olivia   – Why?

Sally   Because one of you drew it, didn't you?
The Gloriana sign.

Olivia   Why would we do that? Why would we risk our lives? –

Ingrid   – Yes. Me.

Olivia (*shock*)   Why would you –

Ingrid   – because there must be something better than this.

Sally   Why did you write it down?

Ingrid   It's not real unless it's recorded.

Sally   Does the bus man know it was you?

Ingrid   I don't think so.

Sally   You don't think so?

Ingrid   I don't know.

Olivia   He'll kill us all if he finds out.

Ingrid   But if the bus man says nothing –

Sally   – you're sure, are you, that no one saw you?

Ingrid   No.

Beat.

Ingrid   What do we do?

Sally   Stay apart. Find a way to leave this place.

Olivia   And go where? The sea?

Ingrid   They say there are other islands.

Olivia   Go out on the sea and we'll die slow –

Sally   – What choice do we have? Separate now. Don't be seen together.

Olivia *and* **Ingrid** *leave.*

Sally *turns to us.*

Sally   How do you balance safety against hope?
   The one who leads, he has kept us all alive.
   Built shelter bare handed, and he alone
   Raises food from the unharvestable sea.
   Each dawn departing with self-salvaged nets,
   Each night returning nets crammed abundant.
   My life, he saved it, does it belong to him?
   And so, at first, our society works.

But there are rules. No citizen welcome
Except those born in what was once England;
And no mention of the girl from the sea:
The girl some say is the hope of the world.
And behind the walls there are screaming rooms,
And within our minds knives are heated white,
In case a thought becomes a spoken hope,
And he who leads becomes sharp he who hurts.
But if you give up hope then what is left?
I am only the world I dream possible,
And without my dreams there will be no me.
So for now our hopes must be deep divers,
Scuttling things surviving the ocean floor,
Secret and held safe far from the surface.

ii.i

Gloriana *on a tiny boat far out in the empty sea. Exhausted, filthy,*
sculpted to skin and bone.

No sounds of the City here: a new soundscape, drawn from the sea.

Gloriana   Day after day I dive beneath the waves
　　Try to slip back to how it began but
　　Where I come from remains a veiled land.
　　What power I had seems gone. I listen:

– Her hands over eyes –

　　Silence. And I am exiled from myself.
　　No longer the sound of a thousand souls,
　　Human sighs now changed for the howl of whales,
　　The shriek of gulls, honest ancient chorus.
　　I am alone.
　　Like a mystic platformed high in the desert.
　　I am alone.
　　I am taken far out to sea so I dream,
　　Dream first of different lives I once heard;
　　My hair could have been piled high scented clean

My skin smoothed buttermilk and coconut;
A little house, thousand miles from the sea
Fields all green and safe stretching clear away
And in that house my beloved O my heart

Now **Kathryn**'s *face projected on water.*

And in my dream days become weeks and weeks
Months and then we are grey and old together
Her arms around me a little O the earth
And that life, that simple life it is so good
And then that is dreamed and that is done, gone.

Kathryn's *face gone*

Then my dreams like water coalescing
form new faces and I know that I walk
through memory, through the land of the dead

Now **Jack**'s *face on the water.*

What do you want? What do you want from me?
If I could have done more then tell me what!
I do not want to return to the world.
Here I live safe cocooned and you cannot
Promise if I return the sun will rise.
I will not be me for you. I will not!
I will cut out of me that part you want –

Gloriana *takes the knife she found in Part Three. Deliberately she cuts the tattoos from her fingers, gouging out flesh. Blood-drenched hands. Gulping breaths. Wraps a rag around them. She sinks back onto her platform.*

ii.ii

Albion Island.

A Perspex container, like a huge fish tank, nearly full of water.

Sally *and* **Ingrid** *and* **Olivia** *stand by the sea, conscious of being overheard.*

Sally   You have water? Food?

Olivia   We have some.

Sally   When they are doing the killing, we go. They will be distracted then. Take three boats –

Ingrid   Why three?

Sally   We go separately.

Ingrid   We go alone?

Sally   It will be harder for them to hunt three.

Olivia   Where do we go?

Sally (*shrugs*)   I will go north. (*To* **Ingrid**.) You east. (*To* **Olivia**.) You west.

Olivia   How do we know there are other islands out there?

Sally   We hope. Now quiet, and be ready –

Enter the residents of Albion Island.

The **Bus Man** *being lead, hands tied.* **Sam** *amongst the crowd.*

Sally *talks to us.*

Sally   They led him out, the condemned man. Hands tied, stumbling. We did not have alcohol for him, to mix with fear. It was a sober fate. If you spread word of Gloriana, the girl who brought the water then we send you to the water. There is logic in that.

The man held by the side of the tank now.

Sally   No last words allowed.

The **Bus Man** *is placed in the tank, the water at his shoulders.*

Sally   Now more water poured in.

The tank is filled with water, rising above the **Bus Man**'s *head.*

Sally   Always they look surprised, as the water rises over their head. It can't be surprise at the process: we all know what will be done, we have seen it before.

He is struggling now, fighting against his restraints. His moment had come before his story even made sense to him.

I find myself stepping to the front of the crowd, and his eyes find mine. There is water on my face.

The **Bus Man** *drowning now.*

Sally   Why did he choose me, for his last sight? Because of my tears?

Ingrid *and* **Olivia** *leaving now, heading towards the boats, unseen.*

Sally   I felt the other girls leave, as we had decided, without looking felt their sudden unremarked absence. My eyes were just for him.

I could not run.

Because of a barely known man's death would I find mine?

I step closer, looking into those eyes, darkening.

What did he see, as the light dazzled to stars and then to darkness?

His eyes close now and I look across and I see Sam, and there are tears on his face.

Sam *watching the dying.*

Sally   Did Sam weep for a man's death? Or was it the sweet violence of the scene, a tyrant weeping at his perfect art, blood red symmetry of crime and punishment?

The **Bus Man** *dies.*

Sally   Turning away Sam sees me, my tears fresh, mirroring his own.

It is over now. My moment to flee passing with the drownded man.

Focus: **Ingrid** *and* **Olivia** *leaving on little boats and heading separate out onto the empty sea.*

– time passing –

ii.iii

Olivia*, on her boat, exhausted and starving, moving through night mist.*

Olivia   I do not know how long I travelled, how many days and nights. My skin burnt by the sun, stolen water long drunk, stolen food gone. I knew I would die, alone, out among the waves. It was alright, really it was alright. So many gone already –

Now little boats in a perimeter line, each with one occupant.

Olivia   And then I saw little boats, like ghosts hanging in mist, strung out in a line. And in each boat a single figure stood. Sentries? Do I call out? Should I be afraid? I crouch down in my boat. But their eyes look inward, they did not seem to see me as I passed. And then one solitary boatman started a low moan, a cry of deep sorrow.

These sounds of sorrow.

This sound going on and on and then suddenly silent. And then from the next boat the same sound, a sadness passed down this long chain. And then that boat falling silent and the sorrow wailed out from the next boat and then the next.

Now she passes through the perimeter line of little boats, and approaches Renaissance Island.

Olivia   I passed through the line, through these howling waters.

And in front of me an island rising from the empty sea –

Man A *is standing on the shore line. He calls out to* **Olivia**.

Man A   Have you come to join us?

Olivia   Where am I?

Man A   Renaissance Island. You are welcome here.

Olivia   I am?

Your guards, they did not see me.

Man A   They are not guards. They were not there, really. They were in the past.

Olivia   The past?

Man A   Our leader, it is her idea. When the grief for what we lost gets too great, we go out, one by one, into the boats. To the sea. We are not allowed to grieve within the city. Within the city we must look only forward. It is the law.

Olivia   Who makes the law here?

Man A   I will take you to her.

ii.iv

Albion Island.

Sam *sits, waiting, by the sea. Sharpening a makeshift knife. Enter* **Sally**, *afraid.*

Sally   You sent for me?

Sam   Yeah.

Beat.

Sam   The girls, they were your friends.

Sally   The ones that ran?

Sam   Yes.

Sally   I knew them. We all knew them –

Sam   I thought they were your friends. Particularly.

Sally   I'm a bit older.

Sam   Knew them before the wave?

Sally   Everyone I knew died.

Beat.

Sam   Will you sit?

Sally   Yes.

She sits.

Sam   Who were you before?

Sally   Student.

Sam   City by the Sea?

Sally   Yeah.

Sam   What you learn?

Sally   Not much. (*Smiles.*) First year.

Sam   Your friends –

Sally   – they weren't my friends –

Sam   – the ones who ran. Why do they love her?

Sally   Her?

Sam   The girl.

Sally (*to us*)   There was a shake in his hand, the hand that held the knife.

Sam   Really. Why do they love her? You're free to speak.

Sally (*awkward, afraid*)   She means different things to different people.

Sam   What does she mean to them?

Sally   I don't know –

Sam   – They went out to die on the sea for her –

Sally   – Hope. She means Hope. To them.

Sam (*hurt*)   Why? They know she brought this, they know she brought the rain –

Sally (*Shrugs.*)   Yes.

Sam   – Then why would they –

Sally (*to us*)   I lean forward and put my hand on his. The tremor and the knife still there.

(*to* **Sam**) They're gone now.

Sam   They'll die out there. I know the sea. They'll die.

Sally (*to us*)   And I leaned in to kiss him.

She kisses him. He accepts the kiss for a moment and then steps away, shocked somehow.

Sam   Why'd you do that?

Sally (*to* **Sam**)   You saved my life.

(*to us*) And I saw how I might save it again, myself.

Sam   What do you want?

Sally   We're still alive, aren't we?

Sam   They were your friends?

Sally   You saved my life.

She walks towards him, kisses him. And he responds, suddenly pulling savage at her clothes.

Sam   No one must know. I lead. No one must –

Sally   – No one. No one can know –

They kiss, sink to the floor.

Sally (*to us*) Later, deep into the dark night, I wake.

He is watching me. Corner of the room. Is this all just an interrogator's game? Am I to be dragged, one morning soon, to the drowning water?

Silence. His eyes looking deep into mine.

And he *smiles*. And suddenly he is young. He smiles. I had never seen him smile before, and –

Sam   – Are you cold? There is another blanket somewhere. I could get it –

Sally   – No.

Sam   Ok. Sleep. I will watch.

Sally   For what?

And he smiles again.

Sam   A habit. Sleep.

Sally (*to us*)   I watched a man fall in love with a me that was not me.

I closed my eyes. I felt safe.

ii.v

Ingrid, *in her little boat, alone on the sea.*

Ingrid   I went east, as I had promised. Always east, towards the rising sun.

Fast at first, demons behind me, until the little fuel was gone. And then paddling, howling, tongue swollen, starved, mad. My little boat taking on water. Not long left now, for me.

And on the third day, an empty vessel.

An empty boat, floating.

Ingrid   Hello!

Nothing.

Hello! Help me! Help me! I'm dying!

She rams her boat gently into the empty vessel. She's exhausted.

Ingrid   There's a line stretching down from the empty boat
into the sea. Fishing line? Anchor? I need this boat. I pull at
the rope, look down into deep dark water. Doesn't shift.
Lean over, pull again, my strength failing. And suddenly a
hand bursts through the surface and grabs my wrist.

Ingrid *pulls away from the water-screaming.*

Now focus to Holy Island.

The inhabitants of Holy Island gathered. Amongst them, **Johanna**.

They are singing, a tune we recognise.

Inhabitants   Born beneath the ocean of all love
  Girl from the sea
  There's a new world, where she made us free
  She came from that ocean, oh my love
  For you and me, for you and me

  Look up at the darkling sky above
  What can you see
  The stars they'll speak to you in beauty
  It's her smiling face looking down my love
  Girl from the sea, on you and me

  Take her hand and dive beneath the waves
  What will you find
  Deep inside the heart of her mystery
  You'll know through her we'll be saved
  O you and me, O you and me

  Now she's been taken far away
  Girl from the sea
  I'll pray to her every single dawn
  And she'll know that she still holds my heart
  Cause I am her, and she is me
  she is me

Whilst the song is going on our focus returns to the boats.

In it, at one end, sits **Ingrid**. *At the other, now, the* **Captain**. *The* **Captain**, *guiding the boats back towards the Holy Island.*

Ingrid   What were you doing?

Captain   Diving.

Ingrid   You were down so long.

Captain   Yeah.

Ingrid   How do you live?

Captain   Practise.

Ingrid   What's down there?

Captain   The City.

Ingrid (*looks overboard*)   Beneath the sea?

Captain   Yeah. Things we can use down there. I bring them up.

Ingrid   Where are you taking me?

Captain   Look –

The boats approaching Holy Island now.

Ingrid   Who lives here?

Captain   Survivors.

Ingrid   Your family?

Captain   I have no family.

ii.vi

The circle of residents of the Holy Island, they sit in two rows.

The row at the front engaging in debate, the row behind silent. **Johanna** *stands, leader.*

Johanna   Tell me: on which points are we agreed?

Resident   Our governing council shall be ten, because she knew she would find ten good men.

Resident   That the sea is holy because it gave us her.

Resident   That she was flesh and blood, not just spirit.

Resident   That all may be loved equally because she loved a woman.

Resident   That she was sent to save the world.

Resident   That although she failed, in her failure she succeeded.

Captain *and* **Ingrid** *entering*.

Ingrid   What's happening?

Captain   They are deciding what we are to believe. What's orthodox.

Ingrid   About what?

Captain   Gloriana.

Ingrid   Why are the ones at the back silent?

Captain   There is not enough paper, to write. They are here to remember. They are the most trusted. What you agree to remember, it is who you become.

Johanna   And where are we divided?

Beat.

Resident   Is she a prophet or part of the Godhead?

Resident   – Which Godhead –

Resident   – Before the wave she said 'we are connected, we are . . .' (*stumbles on the text*)

Johanna   – What is the passage precisely? –

Someone in the second rank speaks.

Second Row (*machine-like, human rhythm gone*) – we are connected each to each like every cell in every body, melded like each drop of water in the great sea.

We are *us* –

Johanna   – That is what she said.

Resident   When she said that did she just mean Christians? Or other followers of the book?

Resident   Does she belong just to the Christians?

Resident   Do you need to convert to follow her?

Ingrid *sits now, listening. Enchanted.*

The **Captain** *turns, speaks to us.*

Captain   When someone dies they become the people who follow them. They are a recollection, agreed upon. They are themselves, to someone else's purpose.

And although it is never spoken this much is felt: Gloriana is dead. From far off we saw the helicopter spinning down, taken by the storm. Gloriana and the woman I love, Natasha, gone into the fire –

Focus back to **Johanna** *and the crowds.*

Johanna *notices* **Ingrid**.

Johanna   You have come to join us?

Ingrid   Yes.

Johanna   From where?

Ingrid   Across the sea –

Resident   – that is a sacred journey –

Ingrid   – There is another island.

Johanna   Where?

Ingrid   Many days West of here.

Resident   What is it like?

Ingrid (*shrug*)   It is a hard place. But there is food –

Johanna   – Do they know the truth?

Ingrid   What truth?

Johanna   The Girl from the Sea.

Ingrid   It is forbidden to speak of her.

Resident   Forbidden?

Ingrid   Yes.

Captain (*to us*)   I watched Johanna in that moment, a door opening in her mind onto a new world.

Johanna   There is only one law here: believe in her and you are one of us.

Ingrid (*simple*)   I do.

Johanna   Then you are welcome.

Captain (*to us*)   Over long days questions of faith become decided fact, bone dry and instantly as powerful as the ancient –

Resident   – Anyone of any faith may follow her –

Resident   – We are linked, each to each, and to contradict this is heresy –

Resident   – The wave will not return if we believe in her –

Focus back to **Captain**.

Captain (*to us*)   I sit apart from these discussions but I have a special place here, privileged like a relic –

Ingrid (*approaching him*)   – it was you!

Captain   Me?

Ingrid   Who brought her up from the sea.

Captain (*taciturn*)   Yeah. That was me.

Ingrid   The Fisher Man. (*Moved.*) Thank you.

She reaches out, lays a hand on his shoulder, then turns away shy. The **Captain** *uneasy.*

Captain (*to us*)   And then, many weeks later –

Johanna   – Walk with me?

They move away from the others.

Johanna   How many boats can we spare?

Captain   Spare? None.

Johanna   We could build some? Driftwood?

Captain   Perhaps. Why?

Johanna   The Girl from the Sea, she came to me last night, in a dream.

Captain   Did she?

Johanna   We must send people out. We must spread the word of her.

Captain   Why?

Johanna   If the wave will not return because we believe in her, if all are welcome within the following of her, then is it not our duty to tell others?

Captain   They'll want to know, these others, will they?

Johanna   Who would not want to be saved?

They look out to sea, silent.

ii.vii

Now, projected huge again, those faces we remember.

Man A   – Me? Then? I was where the politician was – the woman, used to be Lady Mayor. The island was our world, didn't know if much anything else was out there, anything else left –

Woman B   – Albion. Albion Island. That was me. We followed one man, like a king, he kept us safe and we needed safety. He was the one who decided how we would start again –

Woman A   – I lived on the Holy Island. The island where we followed the Girl, the one who was sent –

Woman B   – Everything came through him, everything was allocated by him. He knew how to extract what was needed. Things grew quickly. If the leader is strong things grow quickly. It was fierce but it worked –

Man A   – at first whatever she said, well that went. But then she wanted to bring people in who knew things. For their voice. I was a plumber, before. I knew water. I knew sewage. Important. If a man eats, well, that man he will shit. She put me on the first council and so I had a voice. First time in my life. Then she brought more people in –

Woman A   – it was exciting, to listen to them, as they came up with our new religion. Didn't understand the ins and outs, but it made sense of what had happened. You have to agree a memory if you're going to build a city. And months later, the day the first missionaries were sent out. I was proud. Like we were sending out astronauts, full of hope, across impossible distances –

And now focus back to Holy Island.

The residents of Holy Island stand on the shore. **Johanna** *addressing the crowd –*

Johanna   Go out onto the sacred sea and search for survivors! Go out and spread the word of her, go out and pass on the truth!

Three Missionaries stepping into little boats and heading out to sea. The Residents of Holy Island singing from their makeshift hymn –

Holy Islanders   Born beneath the ocean of all love
   Girl from the sea
   There's a new world, where she made us free

She came from that ocean, oh my love
For you and me, for you and me

Look up at the darkling sky above
What can you see
The stars they'll speak to you in beauty
It's her smiling face looking down my love
Girl from the sea, on you and me

– Time passing –

iii.i

Albion Island, one night, many weeks after.

Sam *and* **Sally** *together. Just them.*

Sam *looks towards us.*

Sam   Didn't know much about love, before. My father he was disappointed. We know why now – one he really loved was the politician. One that got away. Not my mother, choking her life away, unremarked.

(*shrugs*) I'm not moaning, just how it was.

But I mean . . . *Love.*

He smiles to us, like a little boy.

Sam   She is the secret part of my heart, Sally. So secret I didn't know it existed, before. Like there's another chamber in here, unexplored. And I want to give in, to this new feeling.

He looks across to **Sally***.*

Sam   You alright?

Sally   Yeah.

He moves to her, kisses her.

Sam   I try to talk to her, at night. Afterwards. Tell her what we must do to survive, what it's like to be in charge. Feel like I didn't ever speak out loud before.

(*happily conspiratorial with us*) She gives nothing away. Blank face some nights chatting but it's good blank, know there's something proper underneath –

Sally   – Was it just the girl? I know we mustn't speak of it, but was it? Why the weather came?

Sam   We thought what we had was neverending. Thought history was like a film and we were at the happy ending. We forget to protect it.

Sally   So it was more than her?

Sam (*shrugs*)   Well, day she came, very next day, fucking rain started.

Sally   What would you have done? If you had the chance? Killed her?

Sam   If I had the chance?

Sally   Yes.

Sam   I would have killed her. Yeah, I would have.

Beat.

Sally   I wonder what she was like.

Sam   Like?

Sally   The Girl. Probably all dead, people who actually met her.

Sam   Keep a secret.

Sally   What?

Sam   I met her.

Sally   You did?

Sam   My father, who was a bad man, he brought her up.

Sally   The Fisher Man!

Sam   Yeah. Came to us one dawn.

Sally   What was she like?

Sam (*shrugs*) About your height. Foreign but you couldn't place her. Her eyes I couldn't see through them. Didn't want to be one of us I think.

Sally   Tattoos, like they say?

Sam   Who said?

Sally   Everyone, you know.

Sam   Yeah. Covered. Name on her hands –

Sally (*sotto voce*)   – Name on her hands –

Sam   – and like fish skin, all up her legs.

Sally   Was she beautiful?

Sam (*shrugs*)   Don't know.

Sally   Was she . . . magical? When you spoke to her –

Sam   Was she – It's fucking treason we're talking – (*his anger coming*) She brought the rain! She brought the fucking wave! All this because of her –

Sally   – Ok. Ok.

Sally *backing away from him, frightened.*

Sam   Heh. Don't be . . . Don't be afraid of me –

Sally   Everyone is afraid of you.

Sam   Not you. You hear me? Not you.

Sally   Ok.

Sam *leaves.*

Sally *turns to us.*

Sally   First weeks, first months, his touch was tender and his smile unforced, a little boy walking out onto a meadow. But then his mood darkened, his love becoming rough. Silences growing. He did not speak his heart. And then one night he did not come. Saw him the next day in the common place, he did not catch my eye. Did not come to me again the next night. So I rose and walked out onto island –

Sally *walking now.*

Sally   – crept slow and silent, spying through the dark. I heard voices in a shelter at the very edge of our platformed world. And then a terrible scream –

A scream from this new shelter.

Three people in another shelter/area marked off from her: **Sam**, *a Resident of Albion Island and a captured missionary from the Holy Island. The missionary has been tortured.*

Resident   Why did you come here?

Missionary   To spread the word.

Resident   What word?

Missionary   Gloriana.

Sam   Who sent you?

Missionary   The teacher.

Sam   Who's the Teacher?

Missionary   Her name is Johanna.

Sam (*to himself*)   The Iraqi. (*to the missionary*) Is she with you, the Girl?

Missionary (*bloodied smile*)   She is with all of us, even you.

Sam *hits the* **Missionary** *hard.*

Sam   Where is your island?

Missionary   I won't tell you that.

Sam   Burn him.

Resident *holds a burning torch against the skin of the* **Missionary**. *The sound of screaming from the* **Missionary**.

Sam   Where is your island?

Missionary   No!

Sam   Again.

Again, the burning. Again the screaming.

Sally (*to us*)   The screaming went on through the night. Saw him by the water at dawn, strange energy in him –

Sam *approaching.*

Sally   Sam –

Sam   They say you were out of your shelter last night. After curfew.

Sally   They?

Sam   People talk to me.

Sally   I was.

Sam   Why?

Sally   Looking for you. Where were you?

Sam   Trying to keep us safe.

He looks out to sea.

iii.ii

Gloriana *lies, shattered, skin and bones, on her platform/boat far out on empty sea.*

The sounds of whales, of the endless depths of the sea. Her dreamscape.

Now – through the sound world – sudden and returning come the sounds of the city, that noise that we remember from Part Two.

Gloriana *shocked, sits up, now moaning within the noise, her bandaged hands over eyes.*

The sounds of the city growing, the sound of whales replaced by screams like the screams of the tortured missionary.

Gloriana   – No, no, no –

Gloriana *stands. Takes her hands from her face.*

And now vast again the face of **Kathryn** *on the water.*

She knows what she must do.

iii.iii

Holy Island/The Sea Near Holy Island.

The residents of Holy Island are meeting for their council.

Sound of their hymn being sung.

Focus on: The **Captain** *and* **Ingrid** *are in a little boat, not far out. The* **Captain** *uncoiling rope.*

Captain   We put a trail line out, aft. And then weight a guide line, straight down, to free-dive from –

Ingrid   – what am I looking for down there? –

Captain   – you're staying in the boat love.

Ingrid   I want to!

Captain   How deep have you gone?

Ingrid   Diving?

Captain   Yeah.

Ingrid   In a pool, once.

Captain   Swimming pool?

Ingrid   Yeah.

Captain   You stay in the boat.

Sound of the hymn drifting towards them over the water.

Ingrid   It's beautiful, the hymn. Johanna wrote it.

Captain   Did she now?

Ingrid   Yes, from things Gloriana sang in the Detention
Centre –

Captain   Oh.

Ingrid   This is fun, learning new things.

Captain   Right.

Ingrid   Can I tell you something terrible? Before the Wave,
I was shit bored, all the time. Kept wanting something to
happen.

Captain   Well, it did. (*Pointing out to sea.*) – What's that?

A boat is approaching Holy Island, at pace.

Captain   You recognise that boat?

Ingrid   No.

Smoke coming from the boat.

Captain (*understanding*)   No.

Ingrid   What is it?

Captain   They haven't seen it.

Shouting towards the shore, where the singing has grown in volume.

Run! Run!

They do not hear him.

*The fire ship crashes into Holy Island, explodes. Fire spreading
among the ramshackle shelters. Residents of the Holy Island running
in panic.*

*Coming after the fire ship armed men from Albion Island, in
separate small boats or somehow concealed on the burning craft.
There is fighting.*

Ingrid   I know who they are.

Captain   From your island?

Ingrid   Yes. What do we do?

Captain   Nothing.

The men of Albion Island hunting through makeshift shelters of the Holy Island. Burning and pulling out concealed people. Then moments of resistance crushed quickly.

Captain (*to us*)   We watch, concealed in smoke, as the Holy Island is sacked. Survivors dragged out from hiding places. Shelters burnt. Supplies stolen. And then, the smoke parting, I saw *him* –

Sam *seen through the smoke of the burning island.*

Captain   And there was a moment of strange, surging pride before the shame came, because he was magnificent and he was my son. Reduced to just muscle and will, like an ancient warrior, it was my son and he was alive –

Ingrid   – that's the leader –

Captain   – leader? –

Ingrid   – it is *his* island. Where I came from. We must go, we must run, they will kill me if they find me.

Captain   Yes.

(*to us*) I waited one more heartbeat and turned the boat away.

The **Captain** *and* **Ingrid** *leave amid the smoke, unseen.*

iii.iv

Holy Island.

Sam's *men with captured residents of the Holy Island. The Holy Islanders restrained and arrayed in a line. One Holy Islander standing separate.*

Sam's Man   These have recanted. This one, no.

Sam   You offered him his life?

Sam's Man   Yes.

Sam   Ok.

Now **Johanna** *is dragged in.*

Sam's Man   This is their leader. Their teacher.

Sam   I know who she is.

Sam (*to* **Johanna**)   The girl, she's here?

Johanna   No.

Sam   Where?

Johanna *stays silent.*

Sam   She dead?

Johanna   No one can kill her now.

Sam   Why?

Johanna   I have turned her into an idea.

Sam   It was you that sent the missionaries?

Johanna   Yes.

Sam *hits her once, hard, in the solar plexus. She doubles up, gasping. He kneels close to her, almost whispering, concealed from the others, just for her. Examines her.*

Sam (*simply*)   Don't try to talk. You won't be able to for a while. Just listen.

I need you to help me. To tell these people that you have lied. Tell these people she brought the Wave, brought the rain. Save them. I need you to go back on yourself. Then it's done, you and I. It's done, easy. Just say it and it's all gone. Just a few words, now, in public. I don't want us to live like this anymore. I want to be free of this.

Johanna   I will not give her up.

Sam   She's gone. She did not save you.

Johanna   I will not yield.

Sam (*points to the other prisoner who would not recant*)   This one here, look at him. Save him. If you do it, what I've asked, then he can do it too. You'll allow it. That is what leadership means.

Johanna, *considering*.

Johanna   No.

Sam *lets out a long slow breath.*

Sam   Then it's you doing this, not me.

He turns away.

Sam   Drown him.

The other prisoner is dragged away moaning.

Sam (*to his followers*)   The ones that agreed, they come with us. But watch them.

Sam's Man   The teacher?

Sam   Nail her to the door. Burn the island. Kill the lie.

They drag **Johanna** *away, raise her up, nail her through her palms to a door.*

Leave her hanging there, still alive.

The island burning now, smoke rising high into the sky, as **Sam**'s *men leave.*

iii.v

Ingrid *sits on the edge of the burnt-out Holy Island. Thousand-yard stare.*

Now a hooded figure approaching from the other side of the island, through the smoke. It is **Gloriana**.

Ingrid (*afraid*) Who is it? Who are you? I'm not with her, I promise you –

Gloriana   – With who?

Ingrid   The Girl from the Sea, I don't believe in her, I would spit in her face –

Gloriana   – what happened here?

Ingrid   They killed everyone who believed.

Gloriana   – Johanna, where is she?

Ingrid   They left her, amongst the fire.

Gloriana *walks through the shattered island until she finds* **Johanna**, *nailed to the door, seeming dead.*

The rest of the island still burning.

Gloriana *pulls her hood back, reveals her face.*

Gloriana   Help me! We need to bring her body down.

Gloriana *touches the nails in* **Johanna**'s *palms. And* **Johanna** *moans, eyes suddenly opening.*

Gloriana   Help me! She's alive. Help me here!

Johanna *sees that it is* **Gloriana**. **Johanna**'s *voice cracked, all energy almost spent. Barely a whisper.*

Johanna   I knew I would see you again.

Gloriana   What have you done here?

Johanna   I have told the world what you mean.

Gloriana   I don't know what I mean.

Johanna   I do.

Gloriana   This is not what I wanted.

Johanna (*her whispers fading*)   If you mean nothing the water means nothing, the Wave means nothing, and how are we to continue? If you mean nothing then it is just an empty sky –

Gloriana   – These people died for me. You made them die for me –

Johanna   – You are what you are –

Gloriana   – There is nothing left in me but tears, do you understand –

Johanna   – You are what you are. Serve us now. Force the dawn –

Johanna*'s eyes close.*

Gloriana (*to us*)   And she died, Johanna, the self-appointed apostle.

Gloriana*'s rage coming now, sounds of the city, magnifying. And it starts to rain. The water coming down in torrents, putting out the fires.*

Enter **Ingrid***, with others.*

Ingrid   It is you.

Gloriana   Take her down. Bury her, in the sea. Do it.

Gloriana *walks away, towards the water.*

Gloriana (*to us*)   I walk away. Pain, sudden, sharp throbbing through my hands. Kneel at the water, peel away the bandages. I know what I will see.

The Tattoos returned, perfected on her hands.

Gloriana   'Gloriana.'

She watches the water and then looks up at us, defiant.

Gloriana   What none of them know is the sky did not answer,
They did.
What none of them know is I did not stop the rain,
They did.
If I am a prophet raised from the deep,
Then let me tell you what a prophet is:

An antennae reflecting you back to you.
Anyone sent from God is only sent
As a message from the secret parts of us,
Handed from the hidden chambers of our hearts,
And as we are always ourselves so then
We are caught in a pattern repeating
Caught in histories rhyming retelling
Rolling open once more like ancient scrolls,
And like you and like them I am caught in flesh
Imperfect, unsure, scrabbling at heaven.
Pain and sorrow can make a mind a soul
but pain and sorrow can twist it crooked.
On the night sea the way home leads through hell
And so through hell we must go, full of hope
That someday somehow we step free of fire –

Now the **Captain** *approaching.*

Captain   You lived.

Gloriana   Yes.

Captain   It was my son, did this.

Gloriana   Yes.

Gloriana *considers.*

Gloriana   How many are left here?

Captain   Handful. The ones that fled in time –

Gloriana   Then we will need more. Did any of the
missionaries report back?

Ingrid   Just one.

Gloriana   There is another island?

Ingrid   They say.

Captain   Why? What will you do?

Gloriana (*her eyes facing forward*)   What I was sent here to do.

iv.i

The wide sea, far out from land.

Two boats approaching each other from opposite directions.

In one boat **Gloriana**, *the* **Captain**. *In the other* **Natasha** *and* **Man A**. *The boats circle each other, close: a parley.*

Natasha (*to* **Gloriana**)   You've returned have you child? The one they sent seemed to think you'd ascended somewhere –

Gloriana   – I have returned.

Natasha   What do you want?

Gloriana   What threatens mine will threaten yours, one day.

Natasha   Agreed.

Gloriana   I need you.

Natasha   To do what?

Gloriana   Intervene.

Natasha's *dry laugh.*

Natasha   I will discuss it.

Gloriana   Discuss?

Natasha   *I'm* not a god, Gloriana. There is a council. We will discuss it.

Gloriana   Do it quickly.

Natasha   Yes. Matthew!

Captain   Yes.

Natasha   You know what this will mean?

Captain (*avoiding her gaze*)   What needs to be done needs to be done.

The boats turn away from each other, accelerate away in opposite directions.

iv.ii

Sally, *on Albion Island.*

Sally (*to us*)   We saw the smoke rising, out across the empty sea, those of us left behind. Miles high, biggest thing man had made since the Wave. I was afraid.

Later that night they returned. He came to me.

Enter **Sam**.

Sally (*to us*)   Stood silent in the shadows. Filth of violence on him.

Sam   It's finished.

Sally   Finished?

Sam   We're free.

Sally   What did you do?

Sam   Ended it. The lie won't come into the world through me.

Sally (*to us*)   He approaches me, his face distant, serious.

Sam   I learnt something out there. About you.

Sally   About me?

Sam   Yes.

Sally (*afraid*)   What?

Sam   I love you.

It's time to build again.

I need to tell you something –

(*deep pain*) I could have stopped it. The Wave. Before. I could have killed her, but I was weak –

He breaks.

Sally (*to us*)   There was pain in him, fish hooked deep.

I did not reach for him though.

For too long North lay wherever he said it did.

And I had allowed this, I had allowed that lie to endure.

I had lied to live, lied because it was necessary, lied because I had no power.

But it was a lie all the same: and without the lie his rule would not have been possible.

I *saw* him there, that moment, slumped. He had won what little victory he had long ago decided would define him.

But still he was starving, ravenous, and he thought it was for love he hungered. No, it was for magic, for sorcery's sharp point: the hope that comes with transformation.

He took me that night, gentle, adoring; but his hands were not connected to his heart, the wiring twisted faulty.

I'll tell you an awkward truth: I did love him a little. I was like him, more than a little. And I slept knowing this was it, me done, my life was now the lie. He had won.

The next day I woke and left him sleeping, walked through the clouded dawn, started my long day's work.

I was not unhappy.

Sally *walking away from* **Sam**'s *prone body now.*

Sally   I went down to lay out nets for the fishermen.

Sally *jumps down into a little boat, tethered on the edge of the island.*

In the corner, concealed and unseen by **Sally** *till this moment, sits* **Gloriana**.

Gloriana   Hello Sally.

Sally *starts, shocked.*

Sally   Who are you?

I'll scream.

You been spying on me?

Did he send you –

Gloriana   – Come closer child.

Sally   Who are you?

Gloriana   Closer.

Sally   I'll scream.

Sally *ventures a few steps towards* **Gloriana**.

Gloriana *takes her hands from her pockets. Raises them slowly, in front of her face.*

Sally   Fuck off. No. Fuck off.

Gloriana *lowers her hands.*

Sally   You?

Gloriana   Me.

Sally *starts to cry.*

Gloriana   What is it?

Sally   I'd given up.

I believed it for so long, even when they all said you were dead, even when I heard the screams at night, but I gave up.

You're you?

Gloriana   Yes.

Sally   You will save us.

Gloriana (*accepting*)   Yes.

Sally   Why me?

Gloriana   I need your help.

iv.iii

Projected: Faces we recognise from Part Two. Same background.

Woman B   In the months after the Wave our island, Albion Island, it grew so fast. He, the leader, was our legal system, he found our food, he was judge and jury and executioner.

And it worked. But as the months passed into a year, that hard momentum ground to a halt. Is it because people were afraid? We did enough to stay alive, to stay out of trouble but more than that, you kept your head down –

Man A – At first it had been harder, on our island. Slow to make decisions. Slow to come together. Slow to progress. But then we began to grow, quickly. We became a place other survivors tried to get to.

There was a Council, we were all implicated. I was still part of it then, the days after we saw the smoke rising from the burnt island. And she came to us, our first leader and she said we needed to decide who we were –

Now **Natasha** *on Renaissance Island, live, speaking as if to a great crowd but speaking to us.*

Natasha – We were always responsible. When we intervened. When we didn't. We always pay a price. When we step forward, when we don't –

Man A – She wanted us to agree to join the girl and fight. She knew we could not be ordered –

Natasha – What we allow defines us. What we tolerate, that is the world we will pass on –

Man A – And she spoke well.

iv.iv

Albion Island.

Sally, *alone by the sea. Enter* **Sam**, *with men. He is happy.*

Sally Sam!

Sam (*genuine pleasure*) Hello.

Sally Can we talk? Alone?

Sam (*to the men*) Go on.

They leave.

Sam   We don't need to be secret anymore.

Sally   It's not that.

Sam   What is it?

Sally   She's alive.

Sam   Who?

Sally   You have to promise not to hurt me.

Sam   What?

Sally   Promise me.

Sam   I'd never do that.

Sally   She's alive.

Gloriana.

(*to us*) – it was like a spear reaching into the deepest part of him –

Sam   – How do you know?

Sally   She came to me.

Sam   Here?

Sally   Yes.

Sam   She came here?

Sally   Yes.

Sam   You saw her?

Sally   She came to me.

Sam   Why?

Sam *advancing on her now, his anger coming now.*

Sally   You said you wouldn't hurt me.

Sam   Why?

Sally   – The girls, that ran. They are with her now. She thinks I am with them –

Sam *reaching for her.*

Sam   – Have you betrayed us?

Sally   – No!

Sam   What did she want with you?

Sally   My help. To destroy you. What you have built.

Sam   – You fucking bitch are you with her? –

Sally   – I'm not –

Sam   – Why didn't you scream out, why didn't you call for us –

Sally   – She has power, I was afraid, you of all people know that –

Sam   – she was here and you said nothing? –

Sally   – I wanted her to trust me.

Sam   Why?

Sally   Because now I know where she'll be and when. And so do you.

Beat.

Sam   Why did you do that?

Sally   For you. For all of us. You're right: this must end.

Sam   Where?

Sam   A boat, a mile east. Two nights from now.

iv.v

Gloriana *alone on a boat, a mile east, two nights later.*

Gloriana   Even a prophet looks up at the sky,
Selects a single star from that great ocean
And says this one, this one I shall live by.

Sam *approaching in a boat, with* **Sally**.

With him every boat the Albion Island possesses, full of every warrior they have available.

Gloriana *turns to them as they near.*

Sam   It's her.

Sally   Yes.

Sam (*shouting to his navy*)   Don't let her escape.

The boats move to surround **Gloriana**.

Gloriana   You have been searching for me.

Sam   Yes.

Their boats touching now.

Sally   They're close enough to touch. They do not move.

All of **Sam***'s men watching.* **Gloriana** *and* **Sam**.

Gloriana (*to us but looking at him*)   He gazed at me, like Kathryn did, as if through each pore of skin he'd see each cell and in each cell see concealed at last the mystery, to be torn out –

Sam (*to us but looking at her*)   – Not much older than a girl, dirty, hair pulled back, she's nothing, and then the shock of those eyes as deep and dark as the sea –

(*to* **Gloriana**, *indicating* **Sally**) She gave you up, you know that?

Gloriana   Here I am.

Sam   What do you want?

Gloriana   Kindness alone, I wanted that to be enough. But it's not, is it?

Sam   Not now.

Gloriana   I think I know what you want. I'm your sacrifice. You want me naked, nailed to a tree and then all forgiven.

Sam   I want this to end.

Gloriana   I thought about it, alone on the night sea, that I should die for the world.

But no: I will fight for it.

Gloriana *lights a marine flare, raises it over her head. The hunters shrinking from the blinding light. A signal.*

Sam   Put it down!

Gloriana *throws the flare into the sea. Now visible lights from other boats heading towards them.*

Sam's Man   What are these lights?

Every boat from Renaissance Island and the survivors of the Holy Island are approaching **Sam**'s *Flotilla.*

Sally   Sam. It's a trap. Give up now.

Sam   You, you did this?

Sally   Yes.

Sam *howls out in pain. Then moves to* **Sally**, *hits her, hard, sends her spinning to the bottom of the boat.*

Sam (*shouting to his men*)   Fight, stand and fight!

The two navies come together, and a vicious battle begins. **Sam**'s *little fleet outnumbered and outflanked. A battle which descends to the most brutal, basic, primitive hand-to-hand combat.*

Music –

Natasha   And then the chaos of battle began –

Ingrid   – Boats crashing together, men, women screaming out rage and murder –

Olivia   – No tactics just the fierce urgency of kill or be killed –

Captain   – The dead left in the bottom of boats, left floating away –

Natasha   – I had sent so many to war before but I had never seen it –

Sam   – And we were surrounded, outnumbered, outthought –

Captain   – It can only have been a few hours, just a few –

Ingrid   – But it seemed somehow we had always been there –

Olivia   – Seemed that winter came, that I saw snow falling –

Captain   – And still we fought, and winter went and then the spring –

Natasha   – And on the endless struggle under a sky with no sun –

Sally   – And I looked across and saw the Girl, her boat now far apart, her eyes closed –

Gloriana *apart, sounds of the city.*

Natasha   – And we looked down and the waters were receding –

Sally   – The land coming back to us –

Captain   – The boats held fast now in rising mud –

Natasha   – As if we had been fighting the whole of history –

Sally   – And had not noticed that the world was changing –

Natasha   – And then the Girl stepped forward into the fight –

Gloriana *entering the fray.*

Sally   – And she cut through her enemies, remorseless as the wave –

Natasha   – Silent as she fought, silent as men fell beneath her, as the battle was won –

Sally   – At first she cried, cried as she killed, until her anger came –

Natasha   – And she was sinew translated into savagery, blood soaked, blood raged, screaming out death –

Gloriana *raging as she cuts down her enemies.*

Captain   – Until we were left, grounded, choked in mud and filth –

Sam   – Until it was just me and him –

– A pitched battle fought in mud now, **Sam** *facing his father, the survivors boxing* **Sam** *in –*

Captain   Yield! Give up! My son –

Sam *will not surrender.*

He runs at his father, who dodges his first blow, and is then caught by the younger man's superior strength and speed. Finally the **Captain** *is beaten to the ground.* **Sam** *lifting an iron bar above his head to strike down at his father.*

Sally   No!

Sally *places herself between the son and the stricken father.*

Sally   No.

Sam *raises the iron bar again, ready to strike* **Sally**. *And stops. Starts to cry. Drops the iron bar.*

Natasha's *men take* **Sam**. *He is a prisoner.*

Gloriana, *shattered, blood-soaked.*

Gloriana   And the Flood, it was done.

What is left of the little warships returning now, to Renaissance Island.

Gloriana's *boat in the lead of this procession. And building slowly, from the crew of one boat until all the people in all the boats are crying it out, a simple one-word chant, growing.*

All   Gloriana! Gloriana! Gloriana!

The Girl from the Sea, watching this transfiguration, silent.

v.i

Renaissance Island. **Natasha** *stands by the shore. The* **Captain** *approaches them, humble.*

Captain   It's alright here, this island, you've done well.

Natasha   It will be.

Captain   I need to talk to you.

Natasha   Yes.

The **Captain** *unsure how to begin.*

Captain   There's a girl. On the Holy Island. She fell in love. She's 18. She looks like you did at that age. Would find my eyes watching her, jealous. Because once I'd had that moment: once she'd been you, once we'd been them and then we made decisions and now we're fallen, now we're us. And I couldn't look at her. Cause of the anger, growing. But one day soon something just flipped. And I sought her out and there was joy, there was, there was joy because I felt connected. Felt plugged in to all of us. Wanted to sit close to her and say 'I was you once'. Smile. But she'd not have understood, how love changes, how it lasts –

Natasha   – Matthew, I did love you, once. But now we can never talk of love –

Captain (*he kneels, with great dignity*)   I have come to beg for the life of my son. Even if he doesn't deserve it. Even if he doesn't want it.

Natasha   It is not my decision.

Captain   It is. Forgive me, but it is.

Natasha   I cannot.

Captain   It's because he took your girl –

Natasha   – Don't –

Captain   – Say it, if it's true, say it, it's because he took your Kathryn –

Natasha   – Do not say her name! –

Captain   – He killed her. He killed your girl –

Natasha (*her grief coming*)   Stop it!

He reaches for her.

Captain   – If you can't speak it, it will never heal –

Natasha   – It is the city. It is what the city needs, not me –

Captain   – I'd not be big enough to save him, but you are better than me, you were always better than me –

Natasha   I cannot do it.

Captain   We come to this, do we? You and I?

v.ii

Renaissance Island.

Natasha *and* **Gloriana** *face each other, alone.*

Natasha   When I was disgraced, after the wars in the desert, they said power had corrupted. Ruined the best of us.

It hadn't. It did what power always does: it revealed.

And the world was what the world always seems to be: dark and descending and afraid.

So, I ask, what will you do now?

Gloriana   I haven't decided.

Natasha   You are a threat now, not to me, but to us. You know that?

Gloriana   Perhaps.

Natasha   God can't walk among us for long. It will make us mad.

Gloriana   I am not a god.

Natasha   You, little thing, who mean something to everyone and nothing to yourself. I don't need you any longer. You are an anachronism. Even if the rain begins again, even if the wave returns, we are ready now.

I think you were the baby. But you are a soul, grown, now.

She kisses the girl. Steps back, her eyes heavy with tears.

She watches her leave, turns away.

v.iii

Sam, *confined on Renaissance Island. The* **Captain** *enters.*

Captain   Son.

How are you?

Treating you well?

Sam (*shrugs*)   Yeah.

Captain   I need to talk to you.

Sam   About what?

Captain   I went to her.

Sam   Who?

Captain   Natasha.

Sam   Why?

Captain   Your life, Sam, your life.

(*breaking*) I couldn't make her do it.

It's my fault, it's all my fault, I didn't speak well enough, I didn't know the right thing to say –

There wasn't, there wasn't ever anything bad in you, you were this little lad never stop asking questions, me and your mother running out of answers –

Sam   – Don't talk about her –

Captain   – No, I –

Sam   – Don't ever talk about her –

Captain   – I loved her, I loved you –

Sam   But here we are.

She said no, Natasha?

Captain   She said no.

Sam *takes a long breath out*.

Captain   O my son.

Sam   There was someone . . . I liked, loved.

Captain   – Someone you loved –

Sam   – Don't want to be seen like that. Remembered like that, being taken out there. I need you to do something for me.

Captain   What?

Sam   Your belt.

Captain   That's what you want?

Sam   Yeah.

*The **Captain** takes off his belt, hesitates and then hands it to **Sam**.*

Sam   No Dad. You don't understand. There's nothing here'll hold my weight.

Captain   What do you mean?

Sam   You have to do it.

Captain (*understands*)   No.

Sam   You'll have to be silent, or they'll come running.

Captain   I can't. I can't. I can't.

Sam   This is how I forgive you.

Captain   I love you.

Sam   Do it.

*The **Captain** takes the belt and wraps it around his son's neck. He throttles him: a visceral, horrifying act. And when **Sam** is dead the **Captain** rocks back on his heels and howls out his grief. **Natasha**'s followers run in, see the body.*

v.iv

Renaissance Island.

Sally *sits behind a phone, camera, some sort of recording device jury-rigged. The device that has recorded all our interviews that have been projected huge on water through the whole story.*

Gloriana *opposite her.*

Sally   Will you really talk to us? For the camera?

Gloriana   I have a thing to say to you first.

Sally   What?

Gloriana   You're going to be alright.

Sally   Am I?

They've killed him. I knew they would, when I said I'd help you. You can do right and wrong, all at once.

Can we start at the beginning?

Gloriana   I want to tell you a story.

Sally   About where you came from?

Gloriana   No. It's about you.

Sally   Me?

Gloriana   You. One day, not long really but many years in the future, one day you will be grey and old and wise and you will have led, you will have built the world back better. And there will be a city again and you will have seen it rise. One day then, all those years from now a young girl will come to you, eager, and her beauty will shine like the word hope and she will have sought you out because she knows you were here *now*. And she will ask, she will say, 'Tell me about Gloriana, tell me about the girl from the sea.'

And you will put your head to one side and say, 'Gloriana? There was no such person as Gloriana.' And you will smile and send her away unfulfilled but she will be ready for the world.

The story you see, it's not about me. It's about you.

(*precise*) There was no such person as Gloriana.

Gloriana *stands, moves to the girl, kisses her on the forehead.*

Gloriana   It is time for me to go.

Gloriana *leaves.*

Sally *stands, deeply moved.*

After a moment **Man A** *enters.*

Man A   Where's she going?

Sally   I don't know.

Man A   You said you wanted to record things?

Sally   Yes.

Man A   Who will you play this to?

Sally   Ones who come after.

Man A   But there's no internet, no TV, no –

Sally   – There will be.

Man A   How?

Sally   We'll work it out. Did once.

Man A   What's your question?

Sally (*considers*)   What was it like? Before?

Man A   'What was it like? The City by the Sea? It was my home' –

And we are back where we started.

vi.i

Gloriana *walks through Renaissance Island. Stops outside the place where* **Sam** *was kept captive, and where now the* **Captain** *is held.*

Two Residents guarding.

Gloriana (*turns to the guard*)   The Fisher Man. He is to come with me.

Resident   He is on suicide watch.

Gloriana   I know. Give him to me.

Resident   On whose authority?

Gloriana   Mine.

The **Resident** *considers for a second.*

Resident   Your will, Great One.

Gloriana (*to the* **Captain**)   Come with me.

They walk down towards the sea.

A little boat is waiting.

Gloriana   Go to it.

Captain   Why?

Gloriana   I have one last thing to do.

Captain   I mean, why do you think I want to continue?

Natasha, she knew what my son would ask me to do.

Gloriana   Perhaps.

Captain   Then why?

She places her hands over his eyes. He struggles and then yields.

Gloriana   Close your eyes. Listen.

Is this how he hears the world? Does he find pattern?

Sounds of the City.

Gloriana   Beautiful, isn't it?

Go.

*The **Captain** walks down to the boat.*

Gloriana *concentrates, places her hands over her eyes. Sounds of the City. And music, building.*

And slowly the sun rises.

It is the most beautiful thing in the world.

She looks up at it, this early dawn. She smiles. She walks down into the boat.

Gloriana (*to the* **Captain**)   Come on. Take us out to where we were before.

The boat sets off, towards the rising sun. Music.

Natasha, *on Renaissance Island, stands alone. She watches them go and then turns away.*

Captain   I left with her one dawn, the girl. One dawn
Sailing far out towards the rising sun.
Where we are we should not be and yet
Where we are, we are, and on we must go,
What new world lay ahead we did not know,
Eyes facing front, vanishing world behind.
Here she is, a great one transmutated
From the wretched; and I see that true change,
– which is magic – can only live sparely,
can only touch us now and then, a stone
Skimming across the surface of the sea,
Each glancing contact rippling out new hope.
She looking at the water covetously
As if it all might end where it began
Slip down seventy metres in the dark.
Then she looks up and smiles: I sense new faith,
As if deep within she had seen some order.
Out we went alone on the wine-dark sea.

A little boat disappearing into the light.

I would like to thank these below, for their invaluable help with *Flood*:

Peter Marsden and all at Concordia

Hannah Pathak, David Jones and all at Rescue Global

Dr Sarah Bradshaw

Camilla Knox-Peebles and all at Oxfam

Lucinda Giovanni

Dr James Burbidge

Nasr Emam

John Dean

Crew for Calais

Daphne Alexander

and The School of Night

Nb.

Part One of *Flood* can be watched online at flood.hull2017.co.uk

Part Three of *Flood* is available to watch on BBC iPlayer for 30 days following transmission.

Parts Two and Four of *Flood* will be available as Podcasts at flood.hull2017.co.uk

The original music from *Flood,* composed by Heather Fenoughty, is available on iTunes.

Bloomsbury Methuen Drama Modern Plays

include work by

Bola Agbaje
Edward Albee
Davey Anderson
Jean Anouilh
John Arden
Peter Barnes
Sebastian Barry
Alistair Beaton
Brendan Behan
Edward Bond
William Boyd
Bertolt Brecht
Howard Brenton
Amelia Bullmore
Anthony Burgess
Leo Butler
Jim Cartwright
Lolita Chakrabarti
Caryl Churchill
Lucinda Coxon
Curious Directive
Nick Darke
Shelagh Delaney
Ishy Din
Claire Dowie
David Edgar
David Eldridge
Dario Fo
Michael Frayn
John Godber
Paul Godfrey
James Graham
David Greig
John Guare
Mark Haddon
Peter Handke
David Harrower
Jonathan Harvey
Iain Heggie

Robert Holman
Caroline Horton
Terry Johnson
Sarah Kane
Barrie Keeffe
Doug Lucie
Anders Lustgarten
David Mamet
Patrick Marber
Martin McDonagh
Arthur Miller
D. C. Moore
Tom Murphy
Phyllis Nagy
Anthony Neilson
Peter Nichols
Joe Orton
Joe Penhall
Luigi Pirandello
Stephen Poliakoff
Lucy Prebble
Peter Quilter
Mark Ravenhill
Philip Ridley
Willy Russell
Jean-Paul Sartre
Sam Shepard
Martin Sherman
Wole Soyinka
Simon Stephens
Peter Straughan
Kate Tempest
Theatre Workshop
Judy Upton
Timberlake Wertenbaker
Roy Williams
Snoo Wilson
Frances Ya-Chu Cowhig
Benjamin Zephaniah

For a complete listing of Bloomsbury
Methuen Drama titles, visit:
www.bloomsbury.com/drama

Follow us on Twitter and keep up to date
with our news and publications
@MethuenDrama